C
—

C
—
ONE HUNDRED WINDOWS INTO A LIFE OF TRANSITIONS

CAMERON G ZAMOT

Copyright © 2024 by Cameron G Zamot
All rights reserved.

No part of this book may be reproduced in any form or by any electronic or mechanical means, including information storage and retrieval systems, without written permission from the author, except for the use of brief quotations in a book review.

Furthermore, this book, in whole or in part, is not authorized to be scraped, ingested, or otherwise used for the purposes of training, fine-tuning, or developing Large Language Models (LLMs) or any artificial intelligence systems, whether for public or private datasets, without the author's explicit written consent.

ISBN (Hardback) 979-8-9877112-6-2

First Edition.

For anyone who ever felt like a square peg in a round hole.

CONTENTS

The Author's Note	xi
1. Setting 2	1
2. Why Mr. Dave Looks Like He's 50-Something	3
3. Ig-nore	5
4. The Importance of the Written Word	7
5. Day-Old Thoughts	9
6. Marine Band	11
7. Coffee Stop	13
8. Synergy For Two, Please	15
9. Inconceivable	17
10. Data Rabbit Hole	19
11. Plan C	21
12. The Second Cat	25
13. Insufficient	27
14. Knit	29
15. Zoe Clay	33
16. Inexperienced Rider	35
17. Cameron Park	39
18. Dually Noted	41
19. Chocks	43
20. Foray	45
21. Seasonal Labor	47
22. C	49
23. Similarities	51
24. Howard	53
25. Bike Paq	59
26. Enyi	61
27. Beauty in the Brown	63
28. Chief Larue	65
29. Mountain of Damage	69
30. 4/4 Time	71
31. Where Has Your Mind Wandered Lately?	73

32. Redirect	75
33. Wedge/Windfall	77
34. Silverware	79
35. Toward/Away	81
36. The Store	83
37. Bike, City	85
38. Sand Box	87
39. 2023	89
40. Bonus Round: Movie Review of Dream Scenario	93
41. Myrrh	95
42. Sinister | Dexter	97
43. Archive	99
44. Castille	101
45. Forward Movement	105
46. Island Time	107
47. Run Club	109
48. Tourism	111
49. Boots in the Sunlight	113
50. Cool.	115
51. Bedside Table	119
52. Opportunity	121
53. Costco	123
54. On the Eve Of	125
55. Not I	127
56. Indian Summer	129
57. Maine	131
58. Affordable Wealth	133
59. Four Line Book Report	135
60. A.M. Ride	137
61. Saturday St Paddurday	139
62. 34-Syllable Instructable (Without Pictures)	141
63. Dialogue	143
64. The Last Day of March	145
65. Blue Jeanne	147
66. Under the Mulberry Tree	149
67. Leapfrogging East	151

68. Attaq	153
69. Midnight Mac	155
70. Things I Learned on Vacation	157
71. Fluid Dynamics of a Bachelor Party	159
72. The Entrepreneur of the Future	161
73. Self Command	163
74. Fire Escape	165
75. White Trees	169
76. A1, Standard	171
77. Not the Shortest Blog	173
78. Portal	177
79. Doves Coup	179
80. Cargo	183
81. The Table of Life	185
82. Brats	187
83. Urgency	189
84. Garden Gnome	191
85. A Thought-Provoking Passage	193
86. Grayday	197
87. Midnight Masochist	199
88. Nos2lgi2	201
89. Biking Home Before a Thunderstorm	203
90. A Typewritten Blog Post	205
91. Woodsman	207
92. Electric Moon	209
93. Life of the Party	211
94. Acrostic 2	215
95. How to Jump-Start a Soul	217
96. Shinleaf Symphony	219
97. Haiku 42	223
98. Dear friend	225
99. So, what did you learn?	229
100. 35 Items	233
Editor's Note	237
About the Author	239

THE AUTHOR'S NOTE

Hello.

The book you're holding is an accident. It just sort of happened. It wasn't planned or thought out. It was written at the speed of life.

Each chapter in this book is a blog post I made on my personal blog, the caterpillar, between September 24, 2023, and August 24, 2024. 11 months. 100 posts. All in order, right here. My original plan was to publish the first 100 posts I put up on the blog, but those very early entries were really, really, really rough. Yeesh.

Since I was a kid, I always thought the list of "hardest things one can do in their life" was topped by 1) becoming a Navy SEAL; followed closely by 2) writing a book. Funny enough, this book was not that difficult to write. Whether or not that's because writing a good book is more difficult than just writing a book I will leave up to you. Something about the eye of the beholder…

THE AUTHOR'S NOTE

In September 2023, when I wrote *Setting 2*, I felt like I was on the tail end of what was – until then – one of the most dynamic years of my life. I rekindled a very important relationship, made a name for myself, moved from a spare room in a renovated cotton mill into a 250sf loft that was at least my own place, got promoted in my job, finished my first year of grad school, and proposed to the woman I love.

By August 2024, when I wrote *35 Items*, I had moved into a townhome with that same lovely woman before getting laid off from that same not-so-lovely job, experienced the unique and acute suffering that comes with being unemployed, started a business, graduated with my master's degree, got married, built a thriving community of my own, waved goodbye to my brother as he went off to war, spent endless hours under the unforgiving North Carolina sun, and got a job offer from the City of Raleigh.

I spent a lot of time thinking and writing. I spent a lot of time outside. I hurt a lot and I appreciated a lot. I learned. I hated and loved and tried to numb out and tried to soak it all in.

It was a dynamic fucking year. It was a ton of work. But it was so deeply rewarding.

If I die one day under mysterious circumstances, maybe this book will acquire some value. Until then, it's just one guy's account of the negative space surrounding a truly vibrant year of his twenties.

Thank you for spending part of your life reading it.

1

SETTING 2

Rain drops: pitter patter outside the open
    door,
Nature's housemaid stopping by for a routine
    deep clean

Of the ground and air, debris and detritus off
    to somewhere
East of here, downhill from the divide.

The water that's existed since the beginning
And flowed through how many faucets —

Stop. Is that arrogance? To think that
    humanity,
In all our microscopic grandiosity

Has gatekept every drop when we know less

About the bottom of the ocean than about
   Mars?

Probably. But that's just how humans think,
And for better or worse I'm lumped in with
   them.

A timelapse of weather patterns shows a puff
   over the Rockies,
A swirl over Florida, a flow over California

Afternoon storms, hurricanes, ruined picnics,
Rain over parched land, a respite from the
   beating sun.

Rain, rain, stay as long as you like.
Tomorrow, when you're gone, I'll ride my
   bike.

2

WHY MR. DAVE LOOKS LIKE HE'S 50-SOMETHING

Mr. Dave looks like he's 50 something because he has never been out of shape in his life. He turned 72 in August of this year.

He's never not been physically fit. Think about that. Since he was a kid, there was no point – in either his Army or Air Force careers, or his long retirement – where he had excess body fat on his body. This does not come by accident. It comes from lifestyle choices.

He always prioritized cycling. He ran for a while, but his joints eventually said "nah" because of the impact. But he always rode. He still does, at 70 something. Also: he made a habit of lifting weights. Not much, not any huge effort or Arnold Schwarzenegger biceps, just a few dumbbells in his downstairs computer room.

He didn't (and doesn't) eat like shit. Except maybe when he was deployed to Vietnam. He also didn't eat super crazy healthy. Those who know him can imagine how he'd react if you asked if he ate "keto" or "gluten free" or "high carb" or "paleo." Bucket of baloney. Admittedly, he shares his space with a wonderful cook.

But really – he exercises. Today, I looked at my total cycling time in 2023: 554 hours. My conservative bet is that Dave has put in over 15,000 hours on the bike over the course of his life.

Zone 2. Carbon cycle. Flush all the biological waste and debris and cancer and age out of those cells. 15,000 hours at, say, 140 bpm as opposed to, say, a resting heart rate of 70 bpm. That's 63 million extra heartbeats. If a heartbeat signifies human life, he has quite literally lived that much more than us.

Wow!

3

IG-NORE

Vloggers seem to always make videos like "I tried _____ for 30 days and you'll never guess what happened" (tough making a clickbait title without capital letters, tel u whut).

Do bloggers do that? I don't know. But I can do it without clickbait and without a 7-minute beat around the bush before I get to the fucking point. I also do not get much traffic on this site... I made my bed and I'm layin' in it. Anyways:

I deleted Instagram and, near instantaneously, the expanse of newly-freed-up time rolled out in front of me like a red carpet.

Here's another: I can't answer all the memes that get sent to me within a few minutes — and the world hasn't ended!

And another: in a way, I feel less connected to others. Wait for it......... I feel a corresponding increase in connection to who + what is immediately around me. If comparison is the thief of joy, this is simply me turning the deadbolt on my door. It's easier to get robbed when you let the thief inside.

Last one: that particular creative outlet has closed, more or less. But guess what I'm doing right now, at this very moment? Writing, being creative. It takes less time, and I get more satisfaction per minute of my finite day.

Now: time to make my commute over to a new tab on Google Chrome to start my work week. Yeehaw!

4

THE IMPORTANCE OF THE WRITTEN WORD

If you subscribe to the belief that poetry is a useless art form and/or is unworthy of study and appreciation: fuck off and fuck you. This post isn't for you anyways.

For the rest of us: I was sixteen miles into yesterday's ride when I realized why it's more important than ever to be able to write well.

Ages ago, calligraphy was important because if the recipient of a letter got a page full of sloppy scrawl, it wouldn't have the same effect.

Typists emerged as communications technology was being codified. This structural dynamic played nicely with a more rigid format and tone. This rigidity also manifested in the larger corporate culture.

Late Millennials and Gen Z seem to reject some of that rigidity. It seems that they (we) are also rejecting some of the omg r u rly going 2 rite tht stereotypes that they may often find themselves lumped into.

Amid this collective rethinking of authority (as evidenced by the rise of non-hierarchical companies, for example) there are more and more opportunities for leadership and influence across previously inaccessible swaths of both the power and influence totem poles of organization… opportunities reserved for those who can compellingly articulate their ideas in the written medium.

People out there are silently begging and pleading to have someone communicate with them in a way that isn't dry, unseasoned, overcooked corporate jargon; in a way that recognizes they're a human and are talking to a fellow one.

The ability to articulate ideas in such a way, and to do it beautifully — god forbid, poetically — seems to be quite the energy reservoir.

Don't use Comic Sans where you should use calligraphy!

5

DAY-OLD THOUGHTS

$1 off.

Lol.

Entertaining the ideas and "what ifs" around what we'd do if we were other people is an easy way to feel less good about things. If we had other people's opportunities, if we had their relationship or their car or their job or their bank account or their looks or… what if?

Not that it's always a good way to flip things, but I find it entertaining to consider the "what ifs" around how other people would do if they were me.

What about you? How would other people have handled the shit that life has thrown at you? Would they do it more or less gracefully? Would they take it in stride like you did, or would they get totally derailed? What about the things you didn't handle well?

If they got dealt your cards, could they still win?

6

MARINE BAND

One of the things that inspired this blog from the beginning, Kevin Kelly's *Technium*, once featured a post with the following advice. I'll paraphrase:

When it comes to power tools, buy the cheapest set. Once a tool wears out, replace it with a nicer model. If you use them professionally, buy the best money can buy.

I did something similar with harmonicas. I started off with a $6.99 Fender Blues Deluxe in C. Later, I got other keys: G, A, B-flat, D, E, and F. They're alright. Yesterday I decided to get a Marine Band harmonica in C, because I had done some research and figured I'd benefit from having a nicer version, since I play that one the most anyways.

It arrived this morning. Thanks, Amazon.

Fun fact, this harmonica was patented in 1896 and has not changed in design or construction since. First designed by the clockmaker Matthias Hohner in Germany, it was brought over to the U.S. by German immigrants, who then popularized it in Texas. This model of harmonica has reached legendary status in the blues community.

It feels surprisingly light. The metal back has a graceful curve and flare, like an airfoil ready to soar, or the profile of a racecar, or a blimp... depending on how you look at it. The vents on the side help with acoustics and make me want to wail on it. The pearwood comb, finely cut and sanded, sits flush with the brass reed plates, the visible gold slivers pressed between the chrome shell and rose-brown wood comb. All five pieces of the assembly are fixed together with eight tiny nails. The shape feels much nicer on my mouth and the whole apparatus feels better in my hand than the last one.

$50 well spent. Super worthwhile upgrade!

7

COFFEE STOP

One cortado, please.

I said at Iris, after many. At Stick Boy, down south with a nice group—at a South Carolina cafe, on a spirit quest. Once in crisp air at a shop in Crested Butte, a few times at a cafe off a lazy Florida bike path. Once, at Jubala, then back to espresso because cortados ain't free.

The coffee stop: an oasis, a respite, a meeting place, with so many miles to go, but so many behind.

A little caffeine, camaraderie, courage in a cup, because it ain't ever easy. I wish that bean water could understand just exactly how grand it feels to sit and sip
    and chat
    and be almost back.

8

SYNERGY FOR TWO, PLEASE

Syn·er·gy
noun
The interaction or cooperation of two or more organizations, substances, or other agents to produce a combined effect greater than the sum of their separate effects.

The other day Lauren and I ran into my friend Jordan at Jubala. I introduced them and we chatted a while as we finished our espressos. Then Lauren and I hopped on our bikes and headed home.

"Okay, he is handsome."

"I agree. That was the first thing I thought when we met last year."

"It's similar to how you are handsome: at first glance, just a somewhat attractive-looking guy... but the more you look, the better it gets."

I'm thankful, first, that I'm in a relationship where my partner can feel comfortable saying that. I'm also thankful that she too embodies that quality: the longer you look, the more beautiful she gets. I think she was trying to say that about me too. And about Jordan.

I like to surround myself with people and things that follow that same pattern. I also like creating those things. I also like to avoid things that follow the opposite pattern. If I had a dollar every time I saw a pretty woman, only to get closer in some way and realize the tree was not as lush as the forest, I wouldn't be leaving on a business trip today. I'd be getting my toes done by Jeff Bezos on my gigayacht.

I love things that beg to be examined closer: Lauren, the harmonica, Big Red, my apartment, my friends' personalities, my personality, me.

The sum of all fears and disgusts: beauty from afar, cracked foundation up close. Cosmetically and characteristically.

The sum of all muses and pleasures: beauty up close, so nuanced and metamorphic that it might take months or years to see or experience it... but when you do, it's better than all the parts put together.

9

INCONCEIVABLE

This is not where I will tell you the story of how I lost my bag after I got off the plane and found it an hour later after I'd ridden a bus, rented a car, and learned a lot about the New York Port Authority police. Fun convo.

This is not where I detail who went to the dinner, who did not, and how cinematically serendipitous the entire Manhattan evening was. And how both Manhattans felt. And how I knew right there in the moment that this evening would be forever cemented in my memory and life as a momentous occasion, just as superglue always seems to dry on your fingertips before you're done applying it.

This is not the place I wax poetic about the power of saying yes to things — everything, but only the right things — or the lucid dreamlike superpowerful sensation associated with punching above your weight and pretending it doesn't scare the shit out of you. Or maybe that's naïveté.

Nor is this post about vulnerability and the leaps and

bounds that come from baring your soul to those around you, not limited by shame so much as limited by the time and words sufficient to tell your tale…

Rather, this is the place where I write on a slow hotspot connection on a subway trip from New York Penn to Newark Penn (they're different) and tell you that:

The only thing the world cares about is seeing what's in your brain. Is there something good in there? The world does not reward hard work. It doesn't. It just doesn't. It rewards luck and what's in your brain. What you can remember. What you can say. What you can make others feel about themselves. What you can make them feel about you. And what you can teach them. Yes, you can teach them.

This is the place where I say to myself more than to anyone else:

Every fucking setback and disappointment and stomachache call, email, and letter; every raw-rubbed eyelid, tear-drained, Kleenex-box-emptied night, alone, desperate, with your back against the wall—each was a part of the journey. And when the time comes, someone is going to want to hear about it. And they'll be inspired by it, no matter if they outrank you by a bajillion years.

It's not cliche when I say it's all worth it.

Why?

Not because you've made it. Having made it is the boring part.

Because you're making it.

10

DATA RABBIT HOLE

Oh shit, it's 9:20 something and I am still on my laptop crunching numbers, fuckin' ignoring my MBA homework tell you what.

Gotta do that tomorrow after I drive to Connecticut... I don't think I'll have much time though. Also, how the hell am I going to charge my fucking Nissan Leaf for an hour in New York on the way. Oh lawd. Stress!

Yeah so data - I wanted to figure out some numbers for solar + battery install efficiency. Wanna look at the data and see what region is doing the best. Good = low # of person-hours to install a solar system. Talking aggregates of thousands of hours of work in these numbers. Don't forget that.

Went into Tableau, ye olde faithful. Pulled up Conprod (construction productivity, massive table to sort and organize a bunch of dummy raw data about how fast we are installing jobs).

Got aggregate values for the hours per kW metric for

solar + battery for each region (we have 9 across the country, each spanning a few states except California since California is huge) and tracked it back 5 months. Check.

Downloaded the data. Put that bitch in Excel. Cleaned that shit up and holy wowzers that was a pain in the ass. Jackie Chan waiiiiiii???? Highlighted the table and conditionally formatted so that the highest (worst) numbers were red, and lowest (best) numbers were green.

I hit "done."

And holy fuckin' guacamole Batman.

There's a pattern.

11

PLAN C

Ok, this is probably my least favorite type of writing to do—simple recounting of events and/or facts—strictly reportage, no embellishment. However, I think the story is wild enough to merit bullet points and timestamps alone. Then I have to finish doing my expense report...

This all happened two mornings ago. Thursday morning, after my data dive night. The original plan was to drive to Connecticut, visit a branch, stay the night, and fly out of Bradley International the next afternoon.

- 7 am - Check out of hotel. EV battery is at 30%, 60 ish miles to empty.
- 9 am - Arrive at Morristown NJ, plug in my car. Sit in a coffee shop and crunch out work for about 3 hours.
- 12 pm - Get back into car. Battery has increased

by around 12%. 88 miles to empty. 82 miles to my destination.
- 2:15 pm - Peel off the highway in desperation to go try and find a bathroom. Too bad I'm in the fucking car-centric middle earth of southern Connecticut. Can't even piss on the side of the road because too many Americans are busy commuting from their high-paying New York job to their single-family residence in the suburbs. At 12:15 pm.
- 1:20 pm - Turn around and head back to the highway, bladder hurting.
- 1:45 pm - Try and fail to find a charger. Wild goose chase. Comedy.
- 1:55 pm - Finally find a Trader Joe's and take a Godzilla piss after two futile attempts to find an EV charger that is compatible with my car while sweating cold.
- 2:15 pm - Sit down in a municipal library to do some work, since that was the only place with a functioning EV charger.
- 2:20 pm - Realize that the important meetings I scheduled for tomorrow will occur while I'm airborne.
- 2:25 pm - Panic.
- 2:28 pm - Call the travel agency and have them pull my flight up to tonight.
- 3 pm - Get back in the car. I won't even tell you how much it charged up. It was sad.

PLAN C

- 3:02 pm - Call my mother in frustration and desperation, due to the fact that I will run out of battery 2 miles before I get to the airport and don't have the time to stop, search, and charge my battery sufficiently to return the rental and make it to my flight on time.
- 3:30 pm - Look at the map as I sit in traffic. Traffic. Traffic.
- 3:47 pm - Call the travel agency again. "We just talked, didn't we?"
- 3:50 pm - Do a u-turn on the highway instead of waiting in traffic, head back to New York City.
- 3:51 pm - Receive confirmation for a flight out of LaGuardia at 6:30 am tomorrow, as well as a hotel of unconfirmed quality. At least it's near the airport.
- 5:30 pm - Arrive at an EV charger near the water's edge. Plug in after a few awkward re-parking maneuvers in order to get the plug as close to the station as necessary to charge.
- 5:31 - 7:30 pm - Bigggg snack break :) and long walk around the grounds for the 1964 World's Fair. I've always had a fascination with World's Fairs. A park full of people doing fun things in the evening in early autumn. A dance group. A man on the phone. A family walking. Soccer games. Baseball games. Wonder.
- 8 pm - Arrive at the hotel. Yep, it was sketchy.

Don't even ask me about Friday's timeline...

12

THE SECOND CAT

It is a crisp October morning. Last night was the second alley cat of the year. Smaller and colder than the first. Less hype. Fewer people. More fun, more memorable. Stephon and Vance did the vast majority of the prep work, so shout tf out to them.

It was better largely because Lauren was there, somewhat because of who self-deselected from the event, and somewhat because of how I pivoted from the first event—and chose what not to include.

From my perspective, it was a ride to the park, a very short registration session, and a harmonica noodle with Vance on camp chairs for the duration. Stephon was out riding around. Afterwards: a bunch of us rode to Lilly's and ate more pizza than I was mentally or physically prepared to eat.

My writing style seems like it's changed since May 27. I feel like I've gotten a bit better. Maybe not.

But I read the post from May and cringed. Lol. Well, thanks for keeping up with the blog.

Post script: A few of you wonderfully loyal readers have come back with thoughts carried throughout your days and lives that may be flowers blooming from seeds planted via this blog. Makes my darn day.

13

INSUFFICIENT

There's a Black Lives Matter sign prominently displayed on a particular restaurant overlooking the Raleigh skyline. It's been there for at least two years. I presume it was added sometime around 2020, so that would put it at almost four years.

Now, I agree with the fact that Black lives matter the same as I agree with the distributive, commutative, and associative properties of multiplication. I forget when I first read those on a classroom poster, but it was before 8th grade. Is it useful to have those grade-school posters plastered in the math department of Stanford or MIT?

Cam, where the fuck are you going with this?

Is it useful to have Black Lives Matter prominently displayed in your window, when so many of your patrons are the exact types of people who won't look a Black person in the eye as they pass on the street? The types who come down from their North Raleigh McMansion in their Tesla to eat downtown and treat those who live here with insidious contempt.

For the record—Raleigh is very progressive. I like this. I like it how I like smart Stanford postdocs. I just think it's a little useless to include a multiplication poster on the bulletin board in Building 2.

Perhaps it's the cynic in me, but I think there's more you can do. The sign is the low-hanging fruit. It makes you look good, but it's not a statement. It's a bandwagon, a reinforcement, a virtue signal. It's insufficient.

14

KNIT

I like bringing people together.

Wait wait wait! I see you rushing for the exit. This is not a pithy, self-aggrandizing post about community and togetherness and all that bullshit.

I bring people together because I'm an opinionated and overly particular asshole who is very picky about who he spends his time with. In order to not die completely alone and friendless, I choose to bring people (whose time I value) together.

Oftentimes, they also like each other. Yay!

Today was the weekly Tuesday coffee ride Lauren and I started with some friends, which I like to call the Espresso Express. The name hasn't caught on, but the ride seems to have. It's a short, slow roll with people I enjoy spending time with. New coffee shop every week.

At the fuel stop, we went around the table and talked about books we're reading. Green flag.

My current book is *Where Good Ideas Come From* by Steven Johnson. I literally just had to look up the author's name because it's such a standard-issue, unremarkable white name lol. However, his book is anything but standard-issue unremarkable. It's a fascinating exploration of how we reuse old concepts to cobble together new, sometimes revolutionary ideas. 10/10 recommend.

Break break.

My company is massive and quite siloed. What can I, a measly individual contributor, do to help solve that problem?

Well, I can schedule Google meetings. And I can invite people.

Think big Thursday.

30 min meeting: 5-minute intro, 4x 5-minute time slots for presenters, 5-minute outro/recap. Here are the rules:

Invite only. I'll start by inviting 4 people, but then each of those 4 has to invite one additional person to speak. You have to invite someone to speak. That means that the group grows by 4 each week. It also means everyone knows someone in that meeting. 5 min intro is for people to trickle in because we start that first block promptly. No one can interrupt you during your 5-minute speech on whatever you want to talk about. Literally anything. Work-related, hobby, big thought, whatever. 5 min outro is reserved for scheduling one-off follow-up meetings between people who are interested in hearing more from one of the speakers.

This idea has the potential to knit together far-flung groups and organizations within the company. It has the potential to shed new light on old problems. The best part? I don't really have to do any work.

Does this sound like a good idea? Shitty idea? Let me know in the comments. I would appreciate feedback. Brb gotta go get on a 1:1 with my boss.

15

ZOE CLAY

Zoe Clay died today,
and the world kept right on spinning.
We were never close,
only talked a few times,
but from what I could tell,
she was earnest and frank.
Not a "thank you," but "thanks,"
with the rugged self-assuredness
that sprouts from hard times. Then again, so
    endearing
with beautiful hazel eyes, I realized
as I listened to her stories about Jimmy John's
and her dreams of going pro.
She liberally applied herself to her goals
and had an effect like a waft of honeysuckle
on a warm evening

or rooibos on a cool autumn day.
All these wonderful things about her,
and I never told her till just now.
Zoe Clay died today,
and the world lost something.

16

INEXPERIENCED RIDER

"When I was a boy of 14, my father was so ignorant I could hardly stand to have the old man around. But when I got to be 21, I was astonished at how much the old man had learned in seven years."

—MARK TWAIN

I love this quote in part because of the deep irony that at 21, despite having learned so much, he demonstrates so much of the same naivete.

On this blog, I talk a lot about development and where I am versus where I was, where I have been, where I'm going.

Today was a blinking yellow light saying, "Slow down, bucko, not so fast."

Long story short: today's ride was made unnecessarily dangerous because of the disorganized nature of the group, folks who aren't familiar with the route, and of course... cars.

Five of us (including Charlie, who was still bleeding actively after getting crashed out by one of the inexperienced riders on the busiest road on the route) stopped at Jubala Hillsborough to grab another espresso and collectively debrief.

At that table, in my red haze of frustration, which I attribute partially to the naivete and dumbassity I very much hold and partially to my Cordero blood, I made an off-handed comment to Lauren. I have since apologized three times for it, because I feel genuinely bad. Bad enough that I have to blog-process it, that's how you knowwwwww.

The immediate results of this comment were as follows:

- From the perspective of everyone else at the table, I magically transmogrified into a literal human asshole.
- Just like iron filings near a magnet, each other person at the table polarized quickly into a neat phalanx ready to oppose and ignore whatever else I had to say.
- That last one hints at the most detestable fate of any would-be leader: everyone stopped listening to me.

This situation reminded me strongly of a similar one, years and years ago, in a quiet conference room at the Naval Academy, where I made a similar blunder.

I'd be the first to say that I've changed so much and

matured and yada yada, become more mindful, meditated, gone through shit and suffered and grown and changed since then. And become a better person.

And I'm still making the same mistakes.

These two truths can coexist. Ol' boy Mark Twain did in fact learn a lot in those seven years. So did I. So did we. But the quote doesn't say that *he* learned a lot in those seven years. No—it says his *father* learned a lot in those seven years.

How much I learn, and how much more I realize I still have to.

17

CAMERON PARK

This marker has been placed here in grateful memory of the happy days when girls and boys of this Cameron Park neighborhood gathered here about this great rock to laugh and talk; where lifelong friendships were made; and nearby and throughout this wonderful park great games were played and sportsmanship was engrained; and the lesson of how to win and lose was learned. Those of us who were here look back with thankful hearts for the blessings of those formative years that have gone with us as we have lived our lives—better because of what happened around this great rock. The years seem to have made it smaller in size than before—but no less great.

1996, BY THOSE FROM THE 1930 YEARS

I found this plaque on a walk last night, tucked into the

corner of a park I've passed through probably 50 separate times since I've lived in Raleigh.

The girls and boys mentioned in this plaque played around this rock in pre-war Raleigh when there were no skyscrapers and it was a big rail depot in a small city. Back when tucked-away urban wastelands hidden in the shadows of the interstate were instead baseball diamonds, community centers, and gathering places. Back in those Depression years when there was nothing better to do than go play with your friends around a rock on a hot summer day.

Can you think of a more dynamic 66-year span? World War Two, the rise and fall of communism, the dot com bubble. Korea, Vietnam, Kennedy, the Beatles.

My grandmother wasn't yet born in 1930; my brother was one year old by the time this plaque went up.

The kid who stood on top of the rock as king of the mountain may have gone on to serve as an officer; one of the giggling onlookers may have raised a billionaire.

How much collective life was lived in those 66 years? And after all that time, they bolted a metal plaque to a little, worn-out rock they climbed on when they were kids.

18

DUALLY NOTED

When the dually steamed around us and then braked hard in the middle of an intersection, my amygdala told my prefrontal cortex to start crunching numbers. When the truck swerved to cut off Kaleb, those calculations told me to get up and around the side of the truck on the other side. Good thing I can react a whole lot faster than it's physically possible to accelerate (or decelerate) an 8,000 lb chunk of metal.

When I pulled up abreast of the truck, I had two exit strategies mapped out. I could tell by both the driver's shouts and the pitch of the engine hum that I needed neither. His anger was no longer being routed through the violent manipulation of his vehicle—he had switched modalities to verbal wrath.

At no point thus far had I looked at him. I rarely look directly at things as I ride, but rather look straight at the road and perceive my surroundings through my peripherals, which allows me to see and process significantly more information. This comes in handy!

Right at the same time I realized he was no longer a physical threat and started turning to look at him, his voice came into focus as he finished the sentence, "...won't even look at me, you dumb fuck!"

Before he sped off, I caught a glimpse of someone I truly feel bad for.

Someone who lacks the emotional conditioning to gracefully react to a frustrating stimulus. Reminds me of a chubby fella lining up next to a marathoner. He might make it 100 yards before he blows up, but the marathoner can keep crunching for another 26 miles. Poor fella's got his hands on his knees by now. Winded. Emotional conditioning works the same.

I feel bad for him because he spent so much money (remember, we exchange hours of our lives for money) on a pickup truck that he doesn't need. He could have bought a vacation, or something for his wife, or invested it in his children's future. He could have bought a bike, or twenty. But the bank bought him a truck, and now he's going to spend the next decade of his life settling up with the bank.

I feel bad for him because he was upset by a couple cyclists who couldn't be upset back (well, Kaleb was upset) because we were too tired from riding 80 miles with the goal of bettering ourselves.

I feel bad for him because he left that situation with nothing but frustration and hatred, and I left it with a story good enough to tell you.

19

CHOCKS

I sat and looked out the window as the other passengers filed back towards me. A ground crew member ferried a jet into the gate next to mine—the aircraft I sat in probably had a similar experience only an hour or two before.

Maybe it's me, maybe it was the mint, maybe it's Maybelline, but when the crew inserted the chocks, it got some brain juices flowing.

Let me explain chocks first before I get ahead of myself. Trying to get better at that:

They're small rubber blocks that prevent aircraft from moving. The chocks are shorter in height than the diameter of the wheels they immobilize.

Naturally, the engineer in me begins to wonder: how much horizontal force is necessary to push the aircraft over the chocks? I could probably figure that out if I had a napkin, the weight of the aircraft, the height of the chock, and the diameter of the wheel. After gazing out the window for the past few minutes at the passing Rocky Mountains, I have daydreamed up a rough heuristic (airplane window math, anyone?) which took longer than any math professor would be proud of:

Assuming: a chock's height is exactly one-quarter the diameter of the wheel, the chock has a square cross-section, the wheel is perfectly round, both the chock and wheel are manufactured out of diamond (to eliminate elastic deformation), and the entire system is frictionless, you'd have a 45-degree reaction force as you accelerate into the chock. This means that you'd have to have lateral force (thrust) equivalent to the weight of the plane to get any forward movement. Really, you have to get up and over the chock, which means that for a brief period, you'd need to put out more thrust than the weight of the plane. Let's assume that the plane weighs 200,000 lbs. I have no fucking idea if that's true or if that's way off base. That's 100,000 lbf of thrust for each of the two engines on this plane. That's nearly full throttle (I think!).

Full throttle just to get over two rubber blocks that are a quarter as tall as the wheels on the jet. A small bump could have a greater effect, you'd just have to remember to remove the chocks first. Hm.

Naturally, the philosopher in me begins to wonder: what are the chocks in life that I can remove?

-- Update, I looked it up before I posted this, and a Boeing 737 has a max takeoff weight of 155,000 lbs, and each engine can only put out 34,000 lbf of thrust. Goodbye.

20
FORAY

An exploration into stream of consciousness writing. I heard it was fun.

Cracks knuckles, deep breath, eyes roll back in head

This hotel has a nice view because people come here for work and are exhausted and sit in their bed and enjoy the nice view. But the view is from the hotel. The real view is on a run in the city where the tourists don't go—the places they call "not a beautiful walk" or a normal, quiet, rundown-ish neighborhood. It's beautiful and cool and authentic and unique in its own way—some glittery glow of the 50's haze is somewhere still baked into the bricks that line the narrow roads up and down the massive monolithic ramp which is the Manhattan Beach bevel: a wedge down to the beach where grannies crisscross the bike path on their e-bikes. Why are there so many grandmothers on this beach? Something feels dead about this place, so soulless but somehow so different, so plastic, so strange. So cultureless, amid the amalgam of cultures. California... the exception. The one odd one out, different and separated and partitioned somehow from the other 49 states. Something maybe about Hollywood—about the huge mass of people, of the Pacific Islander and Mexican confluence—so different from anything on the East Coast or inland. But nonetheless something so authentic, so much of something so nameless and barely out of reach, hidden in the narrow back alleys of nostalgia, tip-tap tapping at what could be, what might have been, what once was. The glimmer of the old possibility; then ahead on the horizon, now somehow behind us yet just as far away. The old hopes, derailed somewhere along the line.

21

SEASONAL LABOR

After a long-ass day flying across the country
and an early morning for Jubala
and an economics final,

I am traveling at 60 mph in the passenger seat of Lauren's car on the way to the Sweet Malick Ring rendezvous in Virginia. The tree leaves look nice.

The other night in the hotel I realized that I'm acutely aware of what season of life I happen to be in, equally aware of when that season changes.

When I was a kid, I knew I was a kid. I really wanted to be an independent adult.

I still remember the awareness on the first day of kindergarten (and 4th grade, and the first day of 10th grade) that I was leaving a certain innocent chapter behind, whether or not I would have said it in those same words as a kid.

During that blissful, reckless, heartbreaking summer after high school... I knew what I was leaving behind.

At the breathless peak of my time as the nation's darling, wearing my summer whites (and sneaking out of them)—I savored it.

As I drove away from the academy, I was so excited partly because I knew that I could do whatever the hell I wanted for a few years, but in the same breath:

Part of what made those three years from 2019 to 2023 so tough and simultaneously slightly less painful was being in the trenches and the awareness that I was legitimately in them.

After I raced my first crit, I knew that a certain season of life was beginning.

Same feeling after my first jam night at Oak City. @jack

The only thing that stays the same season to season is that they're all a bit different!

22
C

Quick, I don't have much time.
The emperor walked around his subjects.
Yellow, red, and green leaves twitched and fluttered.
Flip 100 times and you'll be at the end of the book.
It's been a long time coming.
The title is a triplet, and one is a homophone.
The toothpaste is next to the kitchen sink.
There are 5 leaves on the monster in the corner.
Every story, just the same as when you first read it.
But you'll be able to hold it and mark it.
Being around distasteful people is a good opportunity to practice being who you strive to be,

even if the campfire man didn't reply.
Madness and genius, I read.
I hear their steps.
They're here.

23

SIMILARITIES

Between living with a life partner and holding hands while riding a bike:

- When you take one hand off the bar, you have to give up a little bit of control.
- You're more likely to get hurt doing it than if you're riding alone.
- Slightly different trajectories, but moving together.
- It's a balancing act.
- It takes a little bit of trust and focus.
- It's fun.
- It's cyclical but not boring.

Any others?

24

HOWARD

I squeaked one final time and darkness closed in, just as a large figure slid towards me in the evening haze.

Hours? Days? Seconds? Later: I awoke in a dark, fleshy cage. The communication lines to my legs remained severed. I could tell I was traveling quite fast along a bumpy path. I nosed my way into the crevices in the cage as they opened and closed rhythmically, trying to find comfort.

After some time in the flesh-cage, the apparatus carrying me stopped and deposited me onto a large, rumpled, soft leaf, which seemed to be woven from fiber like the spiders in the forest.

What happened next, you may not believe. Nonetheless, I swear it is true.

I looked across the expanse of my silken nest and up the flat, monolithic brown walls. After a half-hearted, exhausted attempt at climbing them, I realized I had no hope. A figure (which I can only assume was the same one I saw coming towards me on the field) appeared over the slab walls. It lowered into my den a large, warm, smooth rock—clear like a dewdrop, but hard as a stone. Then, another. I nestled myself in between them and the odd leaves which made up my new fortress.

Some time later (a duration I cannot confirm due to my exhaustion) I awoke to the figure (henceforth: the giant) moving the leaves around in my den. The giant left a shallow cup of sweet liquid next to me and closed the walls in once more.

A strange hiss and warm vapor emerged over the next short while. I still do not understand what transpired, but the next time I saw the giant, his coat looked somewhat different than before.

My nest began to move again, similar to my earlier experience in the flesh cage. I emerged onto a plain of similar silky material when, to my utter amazement, I realized I was actually standing on the giant! After some hesitation, I began to explore the nooks and crevices of the gentle leviathan. I had never been this close to another animal of this size, since large animals tend to prey on my kind. The giant had some of the sweet liquid from before on its skin—try as I might, I could not find any nipples, and had to resign myself to licking tiny amounts of the liquid out of a white, fibrous stick which seemed to be comprised of the same material as my strange leafy nest.

After a few licks, I looked up into the giant's eyes, it looked into mine, and for a moment there was some sort of mutual understanding that I could not quite place my paw on.

Just as quick: a click, a thud, and a rush of cold air. A second giant emerged! This one had longer fur than the first and did not seem very interested in me. It only ran its finger (oddly large and soft, with a flat claw, reminiscent of the flesh cage from earlier) along my back a few times, and disappeared as the hiss and vapor emerged once more.

The cabin darkened and a long night commenced. As I explored my nest, searching for exits and tucking in for warmth between the warm crystals, I heard the giants murmuring amongst themselves in their den, high up on the mesa near where they had placed my abode. They moved me, yet again, to what I will call the white room. I believe this is where the hiss and steam came from, but I cannot report that with any certainty.

Despite my instinct to wake up and forage in the nighttime, the exhaustion from the evening pushed me into slumber. There, I experienced nightmarish hallucinations and disturbing visions, which I will try to recount here:

In the dream, the giant emerged from the wood, just as it had that evening on the field. However, this time, I saw glistening fangs and could only see one word seared in my mind, over and over: predator. Predator. Predator. Predator. Despite my squirms and struggles, I could not move a muscle. It seized me and I descended back into darkness as the dreamless oblivion surrounded me once again.

The next vision I remember was of the giant looming over me. I was hiding at the intersection of three large, flat walls—the usual comfort of an enclosed corner replaced with the utter terror of having nowhere to run. I looked up into its giant, malicious eyes and realized that all hope was lost: my time was at a close.

I awoke with a start as the giant opened my den and put more food in. It replaced the now-cooled crystals with new, warm ones and poured fresh sweet liquid into the tiny bowl in my den. The giants murmured amongst themselves, then the long-furred one left with a click, a thud, and a rush of cold air. My den moved once again; this time I felt as though I had been placed into a vibrating cart which lurched and hummed as it moved along, giving me quite a strong sense of nausea which I had not felt before.

My den opened up into the morning sunshine. The giant was over me—he pulled me out and placed me onto the dewy, cool grass. At last! I could find cover, I could dig, I could get into the brush and hide. Most importantly—I had somehow regained the ability to use my legs over the long night.

As I retreated into the cover of the wood, I took one look back at the giant. He seemed so much smaller from a distance. I watched as he picked up my den, which from this vantage seemed much smaller than his torso. The two silky leaves which had provided me shelter overnight looked oddly similar to his interchangeable coat, which he had replaced thrice since our first interaction. The crystal, which he held in his hand like I hold seeds and twigs, had provided me the warmth and comfort I needed to regain control of my hind legs.

He strode off into the morning sun, covering vast distances with each colossal step. I began squeaking once more, hesitantly at first, looking for my family and any friendly rodents to whom I might one day be able to recount this tale... even if they do not believe me.

25
BIKE PAQ

Five friends took a train
Biked and hiked through the forest
A campfire delight.

26

ENYI

Reserved and harmless
Just as a claw that's been sheathed
Almost delicate.

An oyster to crack
Once inscrutable, now seen
By others and self.

Adenine and its
good pal guanine, or was it
Thymine? Exactly.

27

BEAUTY IN THE BROWN

Blue water and white sand
Are nowhere near as grand
As the subtle beauty
Of brown water and leaves, to me.
A lake deep inside the wood,
Where a passing hiker could
Sit on a coast of their own
Between the red, gold, and brown.
A river down the road a ways,
Pass it by most days.
I'd stop if I wasn't so grown
And see the beauty in the brown.

28

CHIEF LARUE

Long ago, when I was a younger man full of more frustration and a hotter temper, I pulled off a truly legendary prank that (to my knowledge, as of a few weeks ago) is still talked about in Bancroft Hall there on the banks of the Severn.

It was Air Force week, and naturally, prank time. Each service academy had its own traditions during the week leading up to a big game. This was in October, so it was Air Force week. Army week came in December.

I'd read an article from 2005 or so explaining how a group of midshipmen moved a sailboat into King Hall, our gigantic dining room. All 4,000 of us could (and did) fit in there for our daily meals. The way the hall was structured was in a T-shape, and the boat had been placed on a giant podium at the intersection of each wing.

That's fuckin' awesome. Imagine that. Every

midshipman walking into the dining hall and seeing a massive boat front and center. I want to do that.

So I did.

Long story short (ask me about it next time we go on a ride together):

I got a bunch of my company mates together and set off in the evening to go steal our booty. The process of pulling the boat out of the water was easy enough. Tilting it to fit the mast under the walkways as we breached the academy walls was a solvable puzzle. Then, once we had parked the boat in the grass next to the dining hall, I told the others to detach the mast while I went around back and snuck in through the garbage chute. Gross, but I'd learned that trick the previous year. Easy money. Unlocked from the inside and walked out into the courtyard and...

Then the mistakes started. I came back outside, and every phone light was on (not stealthy at all, especially since hundreds of dorm rooms looked down into the courtyard we were in...) as they looked for a bolt they'd lost. Oops. No matter—we got it inside the building, reattached the mast so that it went up into the rotunda (which had the nice side benefit of being harder to remove), padded the contact points, took some selfies, and left.

What a fucking legendary night. You should have seen the faces the next morning at breakfast. Thousands of midshipmen milling around for a morning meal... And there is an entire fucking sailboat sitting right there. They had to stand somewhere else for the morning announcements :)

Anyways, snap back to reality now, and I've got to go to work. No, not work as a member of the United States Navy

—I am a civilian (as all of you know). That's a story for a different day. Maybe tomorrow. And maybe tomorrow I'll actually tell you who Chief Larue is and why I used his name for this post title. He's one of the good guys, that much I will say.

29

MOUNTAIN OF DAMAGE

Second (maybe third) un-fun Halloween in the books. We are on a streak! As I approach my 20th consecutive hour in bed, allow me to recount for you the tale I wanted to tell yesterday. I promise I won't get distracted this go-around.

In the wake of the sailboat incident, Chief Larue was the SNCO assigned as the preliminary investigating officer in my case. Since I was the only one in the group of midshipmen who executed the prank to be formally "fried," it ended up being a nice 1:1 in his office.

BTW—"fried" is when you get submitted into the conduct system. When you get the automated email saying you've been formally entered into the system, your blood goes cold, and you start hallucinating in dreams about marching in squares. Or something like that. I don't know.

So, little sophomore me took my miscreant ass up a bunch of stairs and into what felt a whole lot like an attic.

Chief Larue's office or a classroom for defense against the dark arts? Find five differences.

He was a SWCC or Special Warfare Combat Crewman, which means he was the boat-taxi driver to get SEALs to and from their objectives, usually in a riverine setting. Super badass dude.

I don't remember jack shit from that meeting except he treated me with kindness (so shocking that it stuck with me), and he told me one of the most impactful things I've heard in my life:

"You're going to go through some shit here. You need to deal with it as it comes, or else it will become a mountain of psychological damage that will come crashing down on you later in life. I've seen it happen to some of the best guys I've worked with."

Part of me has always felt bad about not getting to serve in the capacity that I originally intended. His affirmation of the gravity of the situation—and, in hindsight, foreshadowing of the events the following year—makes me feel slightly more legitimized.

Thanks for the inspiration, Chief. I wouldn't have pursued many of the creative or athletic endeavors that now bring me joy without that nagging sense in the back of my head that I still have some shit to work out.

30

4/4 TIME

Oh, I know an old singer back in old El Paso.
He used to sing a song or two,
And here's how they'd go:
They'd go one, two, three, and four, said,
Two-step baby with your back on the door.
Out in the street,
Tell me who you will be.
And tell me, do you see her
When you're looking in the mirror?
Said one, two, three, and four, now ya
Made a little money, and you're making some more.
Tell me, do you ever slow down
And catch your breath?
Or will you keep on working
Till you work yourself to death?

Two for you and one for me,
Gotta give up something if you want what you
   need.

31

WHERE HAS YOUR MIND WANDERED LATELY?

Thanks for the question, Rachel.

Cassiopeia looks like the Gatorade lightning bolt.
Raleigh lacks a bike rental service.
It is easy to be a company that takes advantage to make a profit.
Businesses that take care of people to make a profit may be more successful in the new generation.
Everyone seems to think life sucks. Everyone makes it seem like it doesn't.
What is the highest value density of my activities?
I find benefit in continually asking and answering that question, thus finding how to best be "lazy" about something: the most straightforward, the least work, yet still accomplishing the task, sometimes better than if I'd done it the hard way. And I never seem to pick the hard way.

Fretboard fluency comes from fuckin' around, like how bike fitness comes from Zone 2.

Off-season running is nice.

What does the future of my cycling career hold?

32

REDIRECT

The thing about opportunity is... each time it comes disguised as a failure, it gets lazier with its make-up.

33

WEDGE/WINDFALL

I am like the wedge:
Punished, but the hammer does
Not do the splitting.

34

SILVERWARE

Doing what I usually do when things get interesting: stop writing.

It's recorded elsewhere.

12 miles into a day-long marathon, one mile every hour, About to go out for 13 of 26.

I wonder where my mind will wander tonight. Maybe I'll tell ya.

I find solace in journeys that bring me closer to me and, in a way, away from the outside world.

Is that what they mean by going into themselves?

35

TOWARD/AWAY

Anyways, as I made mac and cheese tonight, I found that I needed to say that it's okay, even good, to examine the forks in the road. Not to judge them or say this would have been better or worse than that or I wish it turned out such and such.

But just to look at them. Think about what was on the other side of that fork. So far behind you, the line fading off into a milky haze before you can really see where it goes.

And here you are. Thinking about it.

Now read back up the paragraphs in reverse order. That's what's next. Gotta go.

36

THE STORE

I went to the store
and knocked on the door.

Oh wait—hello!
Before I go on, I implore
you to forgive me for
my absence. I won't bore
you with the lore, just know I didn't mean to
    ignore
you four.

Where were we before?
Oh.

I rapped on John's door,
and he gave me a tour
of the spectacular first floor.

With a wizened look, he brought me to
the ocean of experience, I on its shore:

"Thanks for poking your head in the door
And saying hello. That is how
you move through the world."

37

BIKE, CITY

Biking makes a city better, but how? And can you make it sound less boring than usual?

Here's my completely un-backed-up-by-data opinion:

When you're on a bike, you have to look around you. If you're looking down at your phone, you'll crash. Looking up and around you can have a tremendous effect on how you see the world.

Looking at other people can have the same effect. Especially when you're not looking "through" something. How often are we looking at people through windows? When you're in a car, everything except those in your car is viewed through a window. This might contribute to the increased sense of xenophobia and racism and the "us-vs-them" mentality we see in mainstream culture.

When you're on a bike, you're looking at human beings through the cars they drive. Between other cyclists and pedestrians, there is no such boundary.

Why do motorcycle gangs ride together for fun, but car drivers don't? The car. There is no community found in congested traffic, despite other similarities with a bike ride: humans moving in the same direction at the same speed.

I think there's also a correlation between GMP (gross municipal product?) per capita and the average number of "other unfiltered humans seen daily" per capita. The more you see your fellow humans, the more you recognize them as sentient beings, the more you want to support them and the community. Those desires become actions, and everybody wins. The tide rises.

The opposite is also true.

What, then, of the city planner who drives to work?

38

SAND BOX

I made a box out of wood, as I tend to do around Christmas time. My brother gives me a hard time for my lack of imagination when it comes to this type of gift. He's right. Still, I make 'em every once in a while though.

After it had all been drawn, measured, marked, cut, filed, set, squared, and glued, I stood back and looked at what I'd made.

It was nice.

But it was unrefined. It was crude, despite my efforts to file each piece to fit as well as I could make them. Despite my measuring twice, cutting once, but jacking it up and having to start over with another chunk of the board.

The pieces fit, but there were tiny, hair-thick differences in how the pieces lined up. You had to look close, but they were there, clear as day.

Of course, they didn't fit together. The glue was hardly dry.

So I waited, and when it had all set, I brought it back outside and started sanding.

Every edge, corner, and seam. I sculpted each offset edge until they ran flush into each other, not a gap or a way to tell it was two pieces of wood, save that the grain ran a different way.

I ground it down, abraded the unripe facets till they flowed together like an ornate pie crust melting into itself inside the suffocating oven as it grows a golden crust so much more appetizing than raw dough. A lot like life, I thought, on a walk later that night.

I stood back again. It was less sharp, it was a bit homelier. It was, well, worn out. The marks showed the imperfect workmanship, the nicks and nooks showed that it had been crafted by human hands, not by a machine. It was a gift for someone.

It is lovely.

39

2023

A lot happened. I won't recount it all.

The sun rose on the year and I was alone. I watched its final sunset next to the woman I want to spend the rest of my life with, and around friends I didn't know when 2022's morning frost had yet to thaw.

I got a pay raise and a promotion. Then, I was drafted to an all-star, first-ever special team. Then I got unceremoniously laid off.

There now exist four LLCs with my name on them. When the year started, there were zero.

I met close friends; I decided to distance myself from certain others.

I rode my bike a 5-digit number of miles.

I started running again. I won't say I've fallen back in love; we're in the talking stage.

I cried a lot—for the first half of the year. In autumn, I reflected on why I cried so much in the spring.

I achieved at Intelligentsia. I won a race, podiumed thrice, and catted up. This is rare for me to do... I don't typically achieve very much. Maybe it's because I don't set goals.

I cobbled together some sounds and did internet things which now allow you, with whatever device you're reading this on, to listen to those sounds. Orchid Obsidian—look me up on Spotify. Tell me what you think, I need feedback.

Like Portia, I spun a web of connections and touched palps with many well-connected others.

I got plenty high, but I avoided alcohol except a monthly beer when it was time to celebrate something... Like the end of Intelli. I avoided the ol' ethanol poison like it was the plague, despite the pressure to drink, lol. Plenty of dissonance around that topic, that's for another time.

I flew to California twice, New York, Utah, and Florida —all for work trips. Between that and the sycophantic bullshit I put up with at work (before they yeeted me from the company), I think I can say I had a nice corporate stint. Neeeext.

I made a name for myself, then disappeared for a little bit, then resurfaced in a different part of the pool. People who thought they knew me suddenly realized they knew almost nothing about who I am. Just like it's always been...

I spent money wisely.

I avoided driving a car.

I mended certain relationships and chose to let others fray and crumble.

I opted out of spending energy on certain fruitless endeavors.

I learned four instruments.

2023

I read several books.

I made things with my own hands.

I moved twice. The third address of the year has been the best so far.

But I didn't really change all that much. And I think that's okay.

40

BONUS ROUND: MOVIE REVIEW OF DREAM SCENARIO

Besides *Poor Things* from the other night, this movie is the most on-drugs movie I've ever seen. But it was fantastic.

On the surface, it's a sharp commentary on cancel culture, but its genius is that it is so relatable to the viewer. At least for me, anyway. What stood out to me most was how real—how possible—it all seemed. This is partly just good screenwriting. Partly due to the fact that they shot the movie on film (which really boosted the creepy factor in the creepy scenes) and partly due to Nic Cage's great acting. He did a bang-up job!

I thought it was going to come around and be some type of "live a life worth writing about" narrative, but it never did. It never really looped around to any pronounced bottom line. If anything, I think the moral is to act like the type of person that you want to become. I think I heard that advice somewhere else...

His first mistake was to embrace the attention. The

second mistake was the Sprite deal, as he moved away from what he wanted to be known for. His third mistake was with the girl that night. Aside: that scene was masterfully done because of how cringey it was—all these people hating on it are indirectly saying it absolutely nailed its mark. The farts were perfect.

Anyway. Back to his mistakes: all of those mistakes at the beginning—those conscious decisions to do the wrong thing—are the reasons for the flashback to and from the alternative possibility as they said goodbye before he left for Paris. That part just about got me teared up... Which, when you account for the fact that this was also a funny and terrifying movie, is pretty impressive.

I thought to myself at multiple points: this must be what J.K. Rowling's life felt like for a few years. Especially at the very end with the realtor: "people just stopped talking about it."

The "unbelievableness" and jaw-dropped no-way-that-just-happened and I didn't think it could get worse for him left me wondering what was a dream and what was real. Classic A24 is classic.

Overall, top-to-bottom good movie. I'd recommend it. But it's a thinker's movie, so be ready to go on a walk alone and process it afterward.

41

MYRRH

In the space between a missed connection and
   a reality,
The gentle wave after the bus as it pulls away
   from the stop,
The bleary moment as you break from sleep
   and awake to another day you promised
   you'd never get to,
The tomorrows that became yesterdays,
The means that became ends (and the other
   way around),
Each of us, endlessly tumbling down the
   grassy hill.

42

SINISTER | DEXTER

Which eye do you look into?

I look into the right eye. I can't maintain a gaze into their left eye, no matter how hard I try.

The right eye seems to hold in its folds, lashes, striations, and flecks the person we all want to be. The best of ourselves. The ideal, the hero, the strong, just, and kind. Looking into it projects this someone we aim for.

The left eye seems to hold in its glistening gaze pain, suffering, insult, perversion, wickedness, avarice, envy. It holds the person we all want to hide from the world, who comes out in the moonlit moments of our lives, when the unwatching world lies sleeping around us.

Which eye do you look into:

In a conversation?

In the mirror?

43

ARCHIVE

Sometimes I think about how easy it is to wormhole from today to another through a smell, or a song, or a video, or a stage arrangement reminiscent of a scene that happened several acts ago.

A trip here and there between mouse-colored moments, alone, unexpected, when you can sit and think about when things, and you, were different.

44

CASTILLE

Castille van Leeuwenhoek skidded to a stop and looked around.

The stars twinkled atop the canopy of gray sticks, silhouetted against the glistening night sky. The wind rustled through the trees and up his spine. Those he had been chasing with had seeped insidiously out of sight as they ran through the forest. He was alone.

From somewhere deep under his feet: a subterranean *Crack*. Not heard so much as felt. As if a joint had popped deep below the crust of the earth. The colossal reverberations crisscrossed back and forth inside him; the earth seemed to split from the sky along the silhouetted seams.

He awoke on the incubator floor as the saline solution seeped from the sac, still hanging from its stainless steel hook and into the cracked floor around him. Spreading out in every direction were neat, evenly spaced rows of surrogates. Thousands of them hung, suspended in their sacs, about eight feet off the ground. He had taken quite a fall, according to the ache now pouring into his shoulder. Dim fluorescent lights hung seventy feet above, dangling from the unseen warehouse ceiling. A split and a crack, twenty feet away, as a nearby surrogate's casing failed, and they flopped to the floor, the sac oozing its gooey saline across the smooth concrete floor.

All he knew was: run. Far away.

So he did. He ran half a mile to the door of the warehouse, as bodies fell here and there around him, their woozy inhabitants looking around in a daze, standing up, and running with him. He burst through the metal door and out into the open, cool night. What is out there? The voice compelling him to run hadn't quieted, so he obeyed.

Out in the night air, he crossed a concrete lot, a barrier, and a concrete drainage. There was little security, he thought. Then again, why would there be? He felt the desire to stay back, to help the others, or at least ask if they knew what was happening. Where they were going, or if they knew.

He ran all night. As he ran out into the countryside, the shrubs grew thicker and taller into a dense woodland. He stopped and rested and noticed some others had started to filter through the woods. He did not fear them as they approached. Some walked, some ran, but as they passed him, their gaze wandered down, up, and to the other side of him. Not quite at him. He stared at their eyes as they walked past—as soon as they were abreast of him, they locked back onto center, as if on a gyroscope.

He got up and continued walking with them. They

walked in silence for hours, the only sound the crackle of twigs beneath their feet and the gentle rustling of birds in the predawn.

He started to see the first hints of a glow and began to run with the rest of the travelers. He was chasing the glow. They were chasing the glow. The sun was rising, and they ran towards it, the pace and pitch rising to a whir, then a buzz, then a hiss, then a whistle, then a scream, and then the orange ball peeked over the horizon like a fiery eye opening after a long slumber, the earth seeming to split from the sky along its seams, and...

Stop.

Castille obeyed, skidding to a stop. He looked around.

The forest was silent. He was alone.

Then, deep under his feet: *Crack*.

45

FORWARD MOVEMENT

Reach inside, pull on
something deep inside their mind.
that's the recipe.

46

ISLAND TIME

There I sit, on another island between here, there, and nowhere. Another daybreak without further indication of where I'm going, what I'm doing, or if it will really be alright after all. Another morning waking up with a tiredness in my bones that I'm not sure I merit, yet nonetheless feel as I plant my feet on the carpet beside my bed.

Someone told me that the chaos of your twenties gives way to the smooth sailing of your thirties. Does that mean that you figure things out?
I won't hold my breath for it.
Then again, I'd rather be a twentysomething who doesn't think he'll figure it out
But does—
Than one who thinks he will
And doesn't.

47

RUN CLUB

Tonight I saw eyes I hadn't seen in a while.

Blue and deep. Tragic.

Thin curled lips that knew suffering.

A distinctive nose.

I sat on my perch high in the pines and looked down on a lonely boy reading *Migrations* in a hammock.

Phone buzz, book on chest, face turning up to the sky, now

Hot tears leaking from the corners—streaming down and on to the duff because it wasn't over just yet, and for a moment, he didn't feel so alone.

I swung low over the misty lake as two figures came into view.

They crawled out of a tent after a long and confusing night.

I soared up and over the trees, glimpsed the magnificent

sunrise, then—looped back and saw them standing on the shore, looking back at me.

I shared a November morning with a quiet couple sipping coffee in a Waffle House off Capital.

Through a frosty window, I saw a man and a woman quietly eating ice cream in the cold night. Scoops on me.

I walked past a girl as she crouched and left a jar full of poems on the doorstep as the party rumbled inside. She walked away, but I can't say she cried.

I peered from the mantle as a boy took a call, alone at grandma's on Thanksgiving night. Because everyone else had COVID. I saw him grasp desperately at something just out of reach.

Long time no see. Did you get into med school?

I reflected on the bone-deep agony that comes from being controlled. Then again, if you won't do it yourself... someone will.

How perfection is a chimera, all good things are flawed.

I thought about solitude and suffering and tears as water flowed through the walls around me.

How far away it all feels now.

48

TOURISM

I was in Rebus, doing homework today. A walking tour came in. Introduced the store. Told the story. Had samples.

I looked at the site. Hmm. Two tours offered in different parts of town (that are realistically fairly close by bike, not by walking).

Hmm. What about a bike tour company for new Gen Z-ers (what do you call a 25-year-old?) to explore the city and learn about new places? Try out a sample.

I was also complimented when a friend told me she now second-guessed every time she got in her car since I've started giving her shit for driving when she lives so close to work.

She is also bringing three friends to the Espresso Express.

49

BOOTS IN THE SUNLIGHT

It's fun to meet a node in the network—someone who is a social or communal center of gravity, many little flagella connecting and pairing with others with a manner of voracity not exhibited by those outside the boundaries, whose social gravity is influenced not by deed or stature but by connections.

Ah! Yes— the measure of success in life is different in each season. Does a meeting of a certain measure early on in life necessarily doom those individuals to failing in a wildly different game with wildly different rules to which all of us transition as we grow older?

Connections. Like the "palps touching exercise" done daily with other members of the community from which Portia derives her status in *Children of Time* by Adrian Tchaikovsky.

Hmm.

50

COOL.

Fuck.

The Wells Fargo flatscreen says rain coming in an hour, at 9. The bus isn't till 10:15. Then the 35-minute ride, then the hour walk...

I'm still across town from the station. Guess I'm not playing tonight. Can't have the strings getting wet. So much for that. Maybe I'll stop at Benny's for a slice. It's been better in there since they fired that loud chick.

Work just got off a few minutes ago. It went okay. Wanda was a bitch, as always. At least she didn't bring her kid in today. Miguel showed me some of the new Pokémon cards he's collecting. I don't get why he's into that shit. Isn't that for kids? The cards were cool, I guess. He's cool too, I guess. But I'm tired of working in the kitchen. Get me somewhere else. Mechanic school, maybe. Something automotive.

I duck into Taz's to grab a Backwoods. Slice is sitting nice. A little tobacco and a bench sound mighty fine right about now. Something about greasy pizza... Hadn't eaten since this morning, running late for the bus and all.

I head out the door, bell dings behind me, and I pop around the corner. I've come across town by now, next to the station practically. As I come around, I see a guy sitting on a bench in the middle of the square playing a harmonica.

I head over and sit down a few feet away, unsling my case, and open it. He laughs and says he likes the chef knife I've got on the lanyard when it falls out. I tell him you never know when you need it. Lord knows.

He seems like the city type, but something about him tells me he's not quite. We played a bit, but I didn't have a tuner. We just ended up kind of noodling. Fun. By now it's started to rain. We get under one of the overhangs by the bank. Talk about the city, about Zebulon. The country. Seems cheaper in the city than I thought. Maybe I can move out of Ma's soon.

We get to talking about bikes. He seems like he likes 'em. I tell him about how Ma's house is in the country and I'd bike the miles there and back if I had one. Save me a lot of time. He says he might be able to get me one, give me your number. I'll let you know.

The rain stops for a moment. He says he's got somewhere to be and rides off. I pack up the guitar and sit for a while.

Only five people on the bus tonight. Five of us in a fluorescent box heading down the black road.

COOL.

The brakes hiss and decompress. The bus warbles off into the distance.

I step into the cool night.

51

BEDSIDE TABLE

A long gravel drive.
Aunt and uncle are asleep.
A dark, quiet house.
Dirt path around back,
Moonlit dock on the water,
Strip and jump right in.
Silver sliver moon,
Chins held above the surface,
Breathless and freezing.
Warmth, sheets, a stranger.
Thrilling and ephemeral.
Birdsong outside. Sleep.
A cold morning drive.
Bagel? Only if you want.
Goodbye forever.

52

OPPORTUNITY

"It does not matter that I did it," he said impatiently.

He sat across from me in a blue suit and a white shirt. The room was dimly lit, dark green and orange. He looked at me out of piercing eyes through extraordinarily long lashes. He was pretty, almost. I could see the whites under his irises. The left side of his face seemed twisted into a subtle and involuntary smile.

"It does not matter that I did it. It matters when I did it. I did it when I had the chance. I did it when the opportunity presented itself to me. I did it at the exact moment when I could do it, and not a moment too late. After all, that is the only time anyone ever does anything, no? How can you do something after the chance has passed?"

He went on.

"I found myself in the eye of life's hurricane and took the opportunity to enjoy it for a moment. I dismounted the train in Portland and walked to a pub two blocks down the hill. I had time before the next leg of my journey, so I ordered a drink and struck up a conversation with the bartender. She was a lovely woman. Her name was Madeline. I decided to ask what her plans were for the following day. It was a Thursday night."

"What happened?" I asked.

"Everything, my boy. Life. If I'd not acted when I had the chance, I wouldn't be able to recount to you what I just did. If I'd sat there and wondered, wished, internally debated what lay on the other side of my irresolution, none of those memories would exist. I suppose I would be quite the same man I am today. Then again: my not having lived that story would cause me to be a distinctly different man than the one sitting in front of you right now. The rippling effects of choice and time, you know. It would be a different life."

I leaned back and nodded. The candle between us flickered in its vase.

53
COSTCO

Burbles and boxes
Sagging under their own weight
On a Saturday.

54
ON THE EVE OF

A podcast told me
We remember stressful times'
High def aftermath.

Based on this info,
Memories of tomorrow:
4K UHD.

On Tuesday morning
I found myself in between
Opposite cultures.

Genocide and death;
History doesn't repeat
Itself, but it rhymes.

55

NOT I

It is frustrating that the clearest internal indication of last night's success is the crippling (and, as of 11:32 am the morning after, worsening) sense of *I fucking suck,* as much as I want to be taking a victory lap. Call it a vulnerability hangover, impostor syndrome, or whatever.

I've always been bad at being happy for myself after good performances.

In 5th grade, I played my piano teacher a song at the Teacher Appreciation Day event. I forgot the last half of the song, so I looped back to the beginning and just did the first half again, stopped, took a bow, then walked outside and cried.

When I was accepted into the Naval Academy (my only college application) on the first try, with Presidential, Vice Presidential, and Congressional nominations, I felt neither surprised nor truly proud.

When I graduated with my bachelor's after a long and

hard six years, there wasn't really a sense of impostor syndrome—just genuine surprise at my own apathy toward the situation.

The only times I feel like I can allow myself to be truly proud are the moments after endeavors I only share with myself. A pair of 300-mile solo bikepacking trips: Cohutta Cat and the self-dubbed Columbia Epic. That one 24-hour marathon I did. Many other subtle goals that I steadily tick off the list, without anyone knowing except me.

It's not fun feeling like this. Just another something I get to work on.

56

INDIAN SUMMER

I am exiting the 4th straight hour of overhauling my website user flow. My 500-strong list of liked songs has just served up a tune I haven't heard in years. I pick up my phone and text a friend with whom I shared that song and many memories on the freeway.

Tiny shivers run across my skin, raising goosebumps in time with the escalating crescendo of the song. I sit back and look up, out my window at the mottled gray sky blowing past. I think of who I was when I first heard that song in York Hall, where I thought I'd be, where I am now.

A motivating force: make that Cameron proud. Song is over now. Back to work!

57

MAINE

What would I write of,
What it all really felt like?
Pax Camerona
When life stood up from its crawl.

About weekend trips
About feeling strong and lithe,
Midweek New York trip
Feeling—being—so alive.

Wild hockey games
All the juvenile fights.
Sleeping in a field
On a frigid northern night.

Looking so bravely
At your defining decade.
I look at you now
Staring it down, unafraid.

58

AFFORDABLE WEALTH

The other day I
realized how inexpensive
it is to be rich.

59

FOUR LINE BOOK REPORT

The other day, I finished *Of Mice and Men*. It took me a week to read.

What a travesty, wasting those classics on unappreciative juvenile minds.

Lennie committed some terrible acts—but never from a place of meanness.

Kind people can do terrible, hurtful things. We often forget that nowadays.

60

A.M. RIDE

Ride your bike in the morning.
Go roll around at dawn and feel the earth
    wake up.
Sweat up the hills and fly down them.
Sit, talk, laugh with friends. Drink coffee.
Ride on a Tuesday morning. Or on a Friday.
Go fast, go slow, go long or go alone.
Just ride your bike in the morning.

61

SATURDAY ST PADDURDAY

Imagine how a bee feels when it flies
  Just focus hard and—boom—airborne
  Suspended by his little flapping backpack
  Limbs hanging free, along for the ride
  Aaand—coming in for a touchdown.

There's a party on the porch next door. Someone shouted from inside, "Does anyone know how to fix an Alexa?"
  All, in unison: "Alexa!!"
  I laughed, too.
  Why is that funny?

62

34-SYLLABLE INSTRUCTABLE
(WITHOUT PICTURES)

Remember Mam's quote:
If you got nun nice to say,
Don't say nun at all.

The key to quick wits
Is always being ready
To say something nice.

63

DIEALOGUE

When do you think your savings will run out?
"Whole milk okay with that?"
Don't make me remind you where that money came from.
"I like those glasses."
What if you jumped in front of a train?
"How's the business going, man?"
You numb out every chance you get. Of course, you're getting fucking nowhere.
"See you in a bit. Love you!"
Did you really just post that on Instagram? Jesus...
"It was really great to connect. Is there anything else I can do to help out?"
You could be wiggling your mouse and getting paid biweekly. But no.
"Great job on the event. I had a ton of fun."
You should have scripted your speech. It was meandering and aimless.

"How was your day?"
Funny you ask.

64

THE LAST DAY OF MARCH

Summer sulks in through the screen door
Sidling slowly, imperceptibly
Like a white puff in the stagnant sky.

Summer forewarns its arrival with a warm breeze,
A smattering of yellow flowers where just a few months ago
Lay brown leaves and mud and sticks.

Summer crawls along the walls of ivy
And creeps through the cracks like its colder brother did
In that unrecognizable past we call winter.

Summer whistles and chirps from somewhere
    distant
A stirring rumble of life, so absent
When the city blew frigid and gray.

Summer looms, a shimmering mirage—
Stinging, seething, biting, dripping
As it marches closer each day.

65

BLUE JEANNE

The best revenge is living well
To those who don't already know it:
When you're feeling burned
Rejected, spurned
When your blood boils and your fists furl
And your brain screams "Let me tell you..."
And your brain screams "Let me show you!"
And you scream and cry and shake and shiver
And it all goes into the void—
All you can do is live well.
Keep being kind, keep showing yourself that
You can come out of the flame
Just as beautiful and dignified as you were
When you went in
(Or even more so).

66

UNDER THE MULBERRY TREE

The professor stood before the students, and they paid him no mind. He looked out at them, glazed and elsewhere. In one hand, he held the negative. In the other, he held the positive. Giant industrial prongs protruded from the one. A smattering of onyx orifices into the other. Thick serpentine cables lay coiled on the floor.

As his audience watched, unaware, he slammed the electrodes together. The reverberation lit up the forest in the afternoon light.

So it is to connect two people, he said. No one heard him.

A bright moonlit night, solar eclipsed and waned and went away. The birds all asleep. The metallic buzz of insects in the air. A cement mixer shifts into second and churns uphill in the distance. The faint patter of fingers on keys floats through.

Thou must be like a promontory of the sea—though

against which the waves beat continually, yet itself stands, and about it are those swelling waves stilled and quieted.

Leadership is the art of influencing and directing others in a way that will win their obedience, confidence, respect, and loyal cooperation in achieving a common goal.

Now, I've never led people in a very official capacity. That fast-tracked privilege was taken from me a few years back. I've been relegated to taking the long way around.

In a way, I bet it feels a lot like being a man and turning 40 before you have sex for the first time. Maybe. I wouldn't know. I know damn well I've influenced people, though.

Leading from the front is not a question. It must be done from the front. It can't be done from the back. Doesn't always have to be by the point man, though. You knew that. Sometimes it's not about how fast the leader pulls the group. Sometimes it's about slowing down, maybe? About ensuring that everyone in the train is synced up. Enjoying it. Flowing with it. Maybe not at rest or ease, but enjoying it. There's a difference.

Win cooperation and win. Be a gravitational well of community. That's the goal, although at times the muzzle can get yanked hard.

I'll end with a special fragment:
If you can trust yourself when all men doubt you
But make allowance for their doubting too
If you can wait and not be tired by waiting...

67

LEAPFROGGING EAST

I look at the tiny green hitchhiker and wonder at the similarities we share—both moving through the world at the whim of forces much larger than we could ever hope to comprehend.

A tiny barb snagged on a microscopic filament on my sock. Along for the ride.

The seed is one of my role models. So many opportunities in life present themselves like that fiber: razor-thin, delicate, ignorable. I do my best to hang onto them.

The square-jawed woman on stage held my gaze as she delivered her speech about how much she had accomplished. I was halfway listening, but at the same time quite far away. I held an ear to the ground of my own soul, listening to what it was inside of me that insisted a storm was brewing.

The bell chimes outside.

It seems to me that the world is at war, but I haven't heard anyone admit it.

I bet there was someone named Cameron born around August of 1910. What did Cameron think in the late 1930s when he was twenty-something and reading of rumblings from across the Atlantic? As he stood there reading, what world did he think he would inhabit during his 35th year? How did he think his 40th birthday would look?

Did he feel like me now? Did he think of the last war and ponder what the next war might look like? Will I end up so horribly off base?

History doesn't repeat itself, but it rhymes.

68
ATTAQ

When the click rate drops,
It feels like I'm once again
Writing to myself.

A burst of motion!
Violently decisive.
Then: patient waiting.

69

MIDNIGHT MAC

I returned home after a night at the bar with friends, where we spent hours celebrating Lauren's good news. We parted ways, said goodnight, and rode our bikes home under a waning crescent.

Walking in the door, I vaguely considered going to OCS and weighed how much that would fuck up my life right now. As I put the water on to boil, I considered the implications of the videos I'd seen on Instagram earlier that night.

I wondered if the dull-looking brunette my friend said hi to as we walked out of the bar thought I was an asshole because of my indifference toward her existence (and admittedly overly dolled-up outfit). I silently played out a scenario in my head where I showed her a video of the breaking news before swiping over to my messages, where we'd find a similar video in my family group chat earlier that same day.

As I used the chef's knife to process two zucchinis, some

tofu, spinach, and a block of cheese, I considered how I might feel if it were me heading toward it all. I bet I'd be excited. I'll never know. Maybe they need people like me on the home front. Funny how it all shakes out.

The cast iron sizzled away, and I asked Lauren how she'd feel if her sister was heading out there. The involuntary spasm of the muscles around her eyes confirmed her new possession of a slightly clearer understanding of my internal state.

I drained the pasta and wondered how the war would impact those of us at home. Kinetic wasn't on my list. That is equal parts reassuring and terrifying.

The gooey, cheesy, caramelized meal steamed as the constellation of anticipation, anxiety, and shame orbited around me.

The food was delicious.

70

THINGS I LEARNED ON VACATION

And by vacation, I mean unemployment.

I haven't gotten a job yet, by the way, but the machine is spooling up. Interviews are starting to roll in.

I bet they're rolling in because I learned how to get coffee with people while I was unemployed.

Cam, shut the fuck up.

Hear me out.

Before unemployment, I did this thing where I would sit down with someone I needed to understand and transmogrify into an information Dyson. I'd rev it up as high as it went and suck all the information I could out of whoever it was across the table from me. By the end of it, I knew everything I needed to know about them, and they knew next to nothing about me. It wasn't not pretty, but it wasn't pretty, either.

I found myself on a sofa overlooking Los Angeles from the top floor of a Topgolf, having just finished squeezing dry one particular company vice president. An onlooker to the "conversation"—third wheel-ish situation—remarked with a certain sense of awe on my ability to "do that thing." He was right, I realized. I did it a lot. It was a skill in the same way parkour is a skill: impressive, but there are circumstances when it can look weird.

Unemployment, specifically my efforts with The Bike Library, demanded that I learn to tell my side of the story, and tell it well. It helped me add the other face to the coin. The vacuum was still fully operable and quite employable when I wanted to flip that switch, but I learned to tell my story, show what I have to offer.

Maybe it's the opposite of the typical order of operations you'd see in the character arc, but hey. I think it's been a nice exercise. Plus, buying coffees nearly every day since November has been tuition I'm happy to have paid.

Especially when I get free coffee.

71

FLUID DYNAMICS OF A BACHELOR PARTY

Entrainment is when
fast flowing fluid takes its
neighbors for a ride.

I feel so grateful
to have such wonderful friends
entrained in my stream.

72

THE ENTREPRENEUR OF THE FUTURE

The entrepreneur of the future is fast and uses
    UberEats to deliver 20lb bags of ice.
He animates ideas with cheap tools
Because inflation and wages didn't match up—
Invention's mother is tough as nails.

Cheap tools like Instagram
Or Adobe Creative Cloud: student plan
Or Chat Muthafuckin GPT
Or just...words, carefully placed.

Prime is a simple supplier,
Squarespace does a great job,
And an iPhone is a great cash register.

This entrepreneur upcycles, certainly, but
    knows when he needs a 2x4x8 of pressure-
    treated #2.
Pushed out of the broad storefronts and tall
    buildings—
That's out of the price range and ain't nobody
    helping a white guy—
They find other prime real estate.

Right out of view, under many noses,
For so cheap, you wouldn't believe it.
Lean, aggressive, resourceful.

The entrepreneur of the future is fast.

73

SELF COMMAND

The dichotomy
Of effective self command:
When one, unforced, both

Dictates the bearing
And without hesitation
Sits and grabs the oar.

74

FIRE ESCAPE

I remember it vividly.

The cool blue moonlight falls in through the open window, as we sit out on the fire escape. I watch the New York City street below us hum along in the predawn hours.

The diminishing smell of Chinese takeout wafts through the window as it sits there on the table, going cold.

"Where does Annie think you are right now?"

I don't respond. It all feels so far away. She begins to cry quietly.

I look up at the moon and listen to the mumble of sirens from a few blocks over. A truck rumbles past. An animal in the alley across the street knocks over a trash can.

A few hours earlier, around eleven p.m., we went up to the top of the Empire State Building on a whim. How spontaneous it felt, walking in the ornate gold doors so late in the evening. Coming down the escalator, smiling cheek to windswept cheek after absorbing the breathtaking midnight view from one hundred stories up. The subway hissed and delivered us to the Bronx, the only words spoken by an aggravated man as we stepped onto the platform.

We've drilled so much deeper into the night since then.

It should be a wonderful weekend. Actually, I don't know about that. All I know is that it took a lot of effort to get here. Shit, I got chewed out in front of my platoon for my chit. My special request chit, asking to leave for Baltimore at one a.m. to catch the two a.m. bus to get to New York at eight a.m. It got approved all the way up through Senior Chief, but LT didn't like that, nope no no, so I got to arrive at seven p.m. Climbing up out of the underground bus station was thrilling, probably made sweeter because of the work it took to arrive here. The bus back to Annapolis leaves at three on Sunday. Amir will pick me up in his Mustang, and we will arrive back to the hall just in time to dress up for our end-of-liberty muster. The next day, I will wake up feeling the hangover of a weekend spent shuttling around the Eastern Seaboard knotted in my stomach as I grasp desperately at a semblance of control over my life and emotions.

For now, I sit here and listen to the world go by. I wonder how we've diverged since the start of this mess. We were already moving apart when it began. I never meant to cause any harm; I just continued to move in my direction, and she moved in hers. Now, the tendrils grown together are tearing as we cut away from each other and go off on our journeys.

We will not speak for three years after tomorrow morning. When we do speak next, it will be a request for assistance during the most trying time in my life.

It will be nearly a year after that until we speak again. That will be the final week together, dwarfing the fire escape in time and agony.

I remember it vividly.

WHITE TREES

Tall, twirling white trees.
Featherlike branches reach out,
Circling slowly.

They whisper along—
Longer with each connection—
Under a mauve sky.

The trees grow skyward,
Hoisted high by the power
Of acquaintances.

76

A1, STANDARD

What else do I write
Besides opinionated
And pithy haiku?

Not much nowadays,
Because I have quite a lot
Of things going on.

77

NOT THE SHORTEST BLOG

Today I was on the phone with my dad, talking about a variety of things as always, among them how to diplomatically decline an event invite from a complicated ally. Towards the end, he advised me to "make change in the world, but also make money."

Fair. I do need to eat. This is good advice.

We finished the conversation and hung up as I rolled up to the shipping container shop. My task list for the day was: disassemble the cargo bike cooler section, repaint the panels, stencil them, and let them dry. Then, take the 4x8 plywood sign down, repaint it, stencil it, and hang it back up. Then, reassemble the bike.

I had plenty of time to think. I was only interrupted three times: once by a Mexican lady who currently lives in Munich and speaks not even a single lick of English but who described—in Spanish detail—how much she wants to rent a bike tomorrow (she said I had a Barcelonian accent).

Then, a second time by an adorable young gentleman who was trying very hard to be slick with his date as he begged me to rent a bike even though we technically weren't open (he said he had a great time when he finally returned the bike). Finally, a third time by Benton, who had some spare parts to drop off. (We hung out and closed up together.) Oh wait, one more actually: a firefighter with a dog came by, and during our conversation, he said, "I wanted to start my own business, but I don't have the balls for that."

What I thought about in between those interruptions was this:

On November 14th, I was jettisoned from the trapeze I had been swinging on in the thick darkness of the circus tent we call life. In other words: I lost my source of income.

However, it was like when you jump off the swing set riiiiight as it is going its fastest, right at the bottom of the swing. Maximum speed!

I had all of that momentum for a variety of weird (but legal) life and financial circumstances that allowed me to stretch my period of unemployment longer than I had really anticipated. If you got laid off right now, how long could you live?

Okay, think again. How long? Think again. Hard. Think again. That was (and has been) my life after getting laid off. When I thought a pocket of money would run out, by a variety of weird means, money would show up. Whether from the university for FAFSA stuff, or a tax return, or I sold something, I have somehow been able to not literally disappear from the earth just because I don't have income.

I have a hunch that whatever trapeze rung I will end up

catching is going to be amazing, but far enough away in the dark tent that I can't see it, and gravity only works one way, so I am going to have to spend some time in zero-g.

That's where I feel like I am now. I am flying through space and time, very, very fast and painfully aware that life is a trajectory—not a constant.

This feeling I feel is that of a vicious chase; I'm the antelope, and the claws are nipping at me. It forces me to sprint with all I've got. It forces me to analyze every decision I make, the way I spend my days, the things I think about. It forces me to be my best and to bring my best every day, no matter what style shirt I'm wearing.

In a conversation once, someone said, "It seems like you always are focused on achieving something," and I thought that was funny. It's true. But then again, how can you get kicked out of a service academy and not go to one of the best schools in the country, get a job, then get laid off, and not go and make your own business, strictly to make the story that of an epic comeback rather than a sad failure? Shit, this is like the third Kimbo Slice clothesline knock-out life change since I graduated high school! Man, if I let it end on a bad note (because we are all going to die at some point), that would just be a straight-up sad story. If I manage to make it, it'll be the best story ever.*

It's a coin flip on whether my life will end in tragedy or comedy. In order to minimize my chances of the former, I try to spend as much of my life in a state where a sudden end would classify my time on earth as a comedy.

Do you feel me?

78

PORTAL

The other day, I called a friend I hadn't spoken to in a while and, with all the honesty in the world, apologized for how I acted and for everything that happened between us. He forgave me.

It was very liberating.

It was nearly lunchtime on his end of the line, just after dinner on mine. A strange wormhole, out in the middle of the Pacific, between two worlds. The only thing the same between then and now is my bike, Mason.

I'd never considered living in Raleigh when I dropped my bags in the guest room of his house on Oahu. Based on that one visit, Raleigh wasn't really too high on my list.

A few days after leaving Hawaii, I started my MBA program with an accounting class. That's all behind me now.

I owned a car then. Sold it only a few weeks after

arriving in Raleigh, after flying to Colorado and driving it back. Maybe I'll write about that someday...

I was still on the engineering team. A promotion, a lateral transfer, and a layoff were all still in the future.

I thought harmonicas were toys, and I definitely didn't know how to blow a clean single note.

Bike Library what? Espresso Express what?

Somewhere between fifteen and twenty thousand miles on the bike had yet to be ridden. All behind me now.

Lauren and I weren't planning on getting back together anytime soon. Next week, we're getting

married.

I remember Hawaii as the most oppressively lonely time of my life. Now, I sit in a comfortable abode after a fulfilling day of labor at a company I own, waiting for the woman I love to come back from an evening with friends.

The apology sealed the portal behind me with a hiss and a thunk. The nagging flap on the wound has finally sealed shut. The loose end is tied off.

The kiln has cooled.

79

DOVES COUP

Clayson sent me a snippet of this poem, so I found the whole thing online. Here it is:

The Ladder of St. Augustine
by Henry Wadsworth Longfellow

Saint Augustine! Well hast thou said,
That of our vices we can frame
A ladder, if we will but tread
Beneath our feet each deed of shame!

All common things, each day's events,
That with the hour begin and end,
Our pleasures and our discontents,
Are rounds by which we may ascend.

CAMERON G ZAMOT

The low desire, the base design,
That makes another's virtues less;
The revel of the ruddy wine,
And all occasions of excess;

The longing for ignoble things;
The strife for triumph more than truth;
The hardening of the heart, that brings
Irreverence for the dreams of youth;

All thoughts of ill; all evil deeds,
That have their root in thoughts of ill;
Whatever hinders or impedes
The action of the nobler will; —

All these must first be trampled down
Beneath our feet, if we would gain
In the bright fields of fair renown
The right of eminent domain.

We have not wings, we cannot soar;
But we have feet to scale and climb
By slow degrees, by more and more,
The cloudy summits of our time.

The mighty pyramids of stone
That wedge-like cleave the desert airs,
When nearer seen, and better known,
Are but gigantic flights of stairs.

DOVES COUP

The distant mountains, that uprear
Their solid bastions to the skies,
Are crossed by pathways, that appear
As we to higher levels rise.

The heights by great men reached and kept
Were not attained by sudden flight,
But they, while their companions slept,
Were toiling upward in the night.

Standing on what too long we bore
With shoulders bent and downcast eyes,
We may discern — unseen before —
A path to higher destinies,

Nor deem the irrevocable past
As wholly wasted, wholly vain,
If, rising on its wrecks, at last
To something nobler we attain.

80

CARGO

It's Tuesday, and I haven't worked out in a few days.

In the meantime, I flew to the southern tip of the eastern United States and married my sweet lady.

What a wild story it's all turning out to be. I saw some photos from a few years ago today. Lauren really is the one. I am both grateful and intimidated that I'm part of the family now.

I saw folks I haven't seen in years. We smoked, drank, sat under the waning sun by the pool after a day at the beach, played the harmonica while Lauren and the Colorado ladies splashed with Leo the dog in the pool. Everyone else flew home three days ago, but they are still here because they love Lauren on a deeper level than most, having bound themselves to her during those rare, dark, special days only a handful of months ago.

Our grandmas are best friends now.

I've made my first unofficial "hire." I did that this

evening after an early morning flight back to RDU, a failed nap, a furiously typed blog sent, a carousel created, a typewriter bought, a wheel trued, a kei van driven.

Three days ago: adding to Wynwood's graffiti collection with a travel-size can of Krylon - "CZ ♥'s LB."

Uncontrollably crying as she walked down the aisle. Embarrassing myself on the dance floor. Being embarrassed by my brother during his speech. Feeling very proud and confident and loved by it all at the same time.

Linking friends across memories and lifetimes.

Thinking about the ones I've hurtled through, how many Lauren B will be with me through. Thinking about the unknown future and a past when I would have cared that…

It's Tuesday, and I haven't worked out in a few days.

81

THE TABLE OF LIFE

At the dinner table of life, there are many seats for the unimaginative, the fearful, the risk-averse.
There are many seats for the undisciplined, who need a boss and a stick.
There is ample room for those who dutifully sit down and shut up and spend their days at a job they resent.
There's a reward: it's called a paycheck.
They are always welcome at the table of life.
I wonder: do I have a seat?

82

BRATS

I wonder if a study could prove whether or not military brats go on to be successful because they are so used to change. I imagine that a lifestyle which acclimates you to change is one that prepares you for the inevitable discomfort that comes with steep growth. Being able to change well is the key to success, I suppose.

    I'm writing this via dictation on my iPhone as I sit on a grassy hillside on a sunny afternoon, with puffy clouds meandering along the sky. I feel a lot of unease about my life and future, but I can't help but stop and realize this afternoon is absolutely beautiful. I'm at a point along the cable car line, neither at one station nor the next. Moving along, uncomfortable, scared, suspended above who knows what, but doing my best to enjoy the view.

83

URGENCY

The best thing about life?

You can start doing cool shit whenever you like.

Do something with your life.

Yeah, it sounds adversarial. But I'm starting to realize that when someone says "do something with your life," it's perhaps the most wise and beautiful advice they could ever give.

Do something with your life.

Take your life and do something with it. Do. Take action. Live.

It's really fun. It can take a variety of forms:

Start a business
Go to concerts (or don't)
Date fun people
Find one super fun person
Try drugs (or don't)

Go back to school
Start a family (or don't)
Paint? Go outside? Learn music? Learn a new sport or craft?

What we do in life is the only choice we have. We don't get to choose whether we are born, and we don't get to choose whether we die — that's out of our control. So then, I guess the meaning of life is to…

84

GARDEN GNOME

If we are to stumble into our successes, let us sow our fortunate missteps in the garden, where the sun shines and the fruit grows.

85

A THOUGHT-PROVOKING PASSAGE

If you're considering not reading this entire thing, just read the second and third paragraphs.

The danger is that if we invest too much in developing AI and too little in developing human consciousness, the very sophisticated artificial intelligence of computers might only serve to empower the natural stupidity of humans. We are unlikely to face a robot rebellion in the coming decades, but we might have to deal with hordes of bots that know how to press our emotional buttons better than our mothers do, and that use this uncanny ability to try to sell us something — be it a car, a politician, or an entire ideology. The bots could identify our deepest fears, hatreds, and cravings and use these inner levers against us. We have already been given a foretaste of this in recent elections and referendums across the world, where hackers learned how to manipulate individual voters by analyzing data about them and exploiting their existing prejudices. While science fiction thrillers are drawn to dramatic apocalypses of fire and smoke, in reality we might be facing a banal apocalypse by clicking.

To avoid such outcomes, for every dollar and every minute we invest in improving artificial intelligence, it would be wise to invest a dollar and a minute in advancing human consciousness. Unfortunately, at present, we are not doing much in the way of research into human consciousness and ways to develop it. We are researching and developing human abilities mainly according to the immediate needs of the economic and political system, rather than according to our own long-term needs as conscious beings. My boss wants me to answer emails as quickly as possible, but he has little interest in my ability to taste and appreciate the food I am eating. Consequently, I check my emails even during meals, which means I lose the ability to pay attention to my own sensations. The economic system pressures me to expand and diversify my investment portfolio, but it gives me zero incentive to expand and diversify my compassion. So I strive to understand the mysteries of the stock exchange while making far less effort to understand the deep causes of suffering.

A THOUGHT-PROVOKING PASSAGE

In this, humans are similar to other domesticated animals. We have bred docile cows that produce enormous amounts of milk but are otherwise far inferior to their wild ancestors. They are less agile, less curious, and less resourceful. We are now creating tame humans that produce enormous amounts of data and function as very efficient chips in a huge data processing mechanism, but these data-cows hardly maximize their human potential. Indeed, we have no idea what our full human potential is because we know so little about the human mind. And yet, we don't invest much in exploring the human mind, instead focusing on increasing the speed of our internet connections and the efficiency of our big data algorithms. If we're not careful, we'll end up with downgraded humans misusing upgraded computers to wreak havoc on themselves and the world.

YUVAL NOAH HARARI, *21 LESSONS FOR THE 21ST CENTURY*, PP 72-72

See also: *The Table of Life.*

86

GRAYDAY

It is a gray day. The sky is gray, and I am too. The revenue is dry, unlike the forecast. The past week has been brutally hot and devoid of customers at the shop.

I am adrift in a shimmer of summertime solitude.

The Fourth of July was a blast, but amid the cacophony of friends, burgers, and near-misses with grease fires, I couldn't shake the feeling that I was somehow at the end of the line.

In a way, I guess I am.

Next week, I'll drive my brother and sister-in-law to the airport for a long trip. Lauren leaves on a work trip this week. And next week. And the week after that, too.

Today, I'm reminded of long, quiet, hot summers in the high desert of California, the anechoic days between middle school years on an Air Force base under the blue dome.

I'm in a similar summer now—in-between and at the

end of the line, all at once. Wedged between here and there. There, but nowhere close.

    Adrift on a gray, rainy, hot, humid summer day.

87

MIDNIGHT MASOCHIST

"Another Tecate," Curley said flatly as he lined the fourth empty can up against the wall. The server turned dutifully and disappeared into the red gloom of the pub.

"You realize you could get in trouble with the federal government, doing what you're doing." Curley's gaze bore into George, who sat across the table. George angled away, doing his best to maintain a neutral disposition as he absorbed the words.

"Lennie loves the work. He's always wanted to be part of something like this, but nobody ever gave him the chance. He and I are partners. I'd never cheat my partner," George said, addressing the fan that buzzed softly in the corner of the room.

"It don't matter! He ain't right in the head, and it ain't right to take advantage of him like that. Are you even paying him?" Curley slammed his fist on the table, seething.

George took a breath, turned, and leveled his stare

toward Curley. He looked deep into Curley's angry blue eyes and saw a man who had devoted his life to work. He saw in those eyes the dissatisfaction of never being good enough for his own expectations, never living up to the ideal his father set for him, never being the man everyone always wanted him to be. Curley was tremendously successful—powerful, educated, wealthy, with an illustrious career behind him. But George pitied him. He was crippled. He was sour. He was bitter. His myriad health problems likely stemmed from long hours under the banker's lamp. He was aged deeper than he should be.

"I'm not taking advantage of him. He's my friend. The shop ain't making enough money to pay me, much less him. But he agreed to work together to build something good. We're doing it because we love it. That's all."

The bartender returned with the beer.

"About damn time."

Curley drank the beer in one long swig and added the can to the line on the wall. He pushed his chair back and stood up.

"I ain't giving you any advice. Just giving you something to think about," he said, grabbing his hat from the pommel of the chair. He glanced back as he walked out. George gazed placidly at the rhythmically oscillating fan, his soul clamping down on the war raging inside him.

88

NOS2LGI2

Tiny rocks slide beneath sandaled feet,
    climbing up and over the berm.
Cold water steals breath as young people swim
    across the mountain lake.
Echoes from the other shore reverberate and
    dissipate.
Sun bakes seven sweaty skins on the stump of
    a peninsula.
Summer lies still in the thin, cool afternoon
    air.

89

BIKING HOME BEFORE A THUNDERSTORM

We turn south onto the dark road by the sunflower field in the deep twilight hour. I look up and to the right at the massive wall of clouds. The crescent moon illuminates a few crisp lumps with a pale glow.

Lightning flashes silently down the middle of the wall, illuminating the colossal pile of water vapor. Deep inside the beast, another bolt flashes. The clouds are stacked so high that the last rays of the sun are still illuminating the tops of some. I see the faint orange glow so many thousand feet above me.

At the container, we swap a few parting words. I recommend you start walking now. It's about to come down hard.

The wind picks up, and the trees begin to rustle and pop.

I push hard up the long hill, my blood pumps, and I try to hold my gaze on the sky as my muscles go into debt. Beauty and pain. I look up and see the sky light up again. The clouds have drifted over me by now. I see a haze in the dim sky above me. To my left, I see the deep gray of the leviathan's belly.

I crest the hill, pointing eastward, and see a crisp line separating the ominous gray from the deep blue night sky beyond. I imagine the view from a weather balloon off the Atlantic coast. A thirty-thousand-foot tall wall of electricity and water gliding noiselessly toward you. I imagine the vantage from the south. The long anvil head cantilevered out so many miles. A sentry.

I turn left, northward, and gaze down the length of the long, straight frontier. The wind whips at me.

I'm a mile from home when the droplets start. The electric humidity gives way to fat drops, diluting my sweat-stained shirt.

Lightning bolts begin to crack overhead. I pedal faster through the wet streets, turning corner after brakeless corner, rocketing home and squinting to avoid rock-hard raindrops in my eyes.

I roll up to my porch, slow, and stop. The magic dissipates. It's no more than a rainy evening.

I step inside and hang my bike up with a towel underneath. I've beaten the rain, for now.

90

A TYPEWRITTEN BLOG POST

A letter to my 8th grade self. Check it out on the blog.
   https://thecaterpillar.blog/2024/07/12/a-typewritten-blog-post/

The QR code will take you there

91

WOODSMAN

The woodsman sat, wearing a flannel, on a stump across the clearing from the tall, thick trunk of a spruce tree. Across his lap lay an axe. In his right hand, a whetstone. To his left, the surprising length of what used to be a tall spruce. Yesterday's labor.

The sun's precarious noontime balancing act toppled into afternoon and then evening as the man sat there—motionless, save for the rhythmic passing of stone over steel. The shadows snuck along the forest floor as the birds twittered and squirrels munched.

Tsssssk. Tssssssk. Tsssssk.

His mind wandered to his friends. He thought of all the work and debt waiting for him back in town. All the other things he could be doing. The rasp of the whetstone lulled him into a state of hypnosis. He engaged in imaginary conversations with himself and with people he knew. He saw himself from across the clearing. He continued to sharpen his blade.

As the light turned the color of golden honey, he abruptly stopped and stood up. He turned the blade over in his hand, examining the smooth convex curve of the bevel.

He looked up and crossed the clearing in six strides, finding himself face-to-face with a trunk as wide as his shoulders.

"I'll bet you I can get home before supper."

"You're on."

92

ELECTRIC MOON

Ten friends drink and smoke
Under a lamp by the tracks
On a summer night.

93

LIFE OF THE PARTY

When I was little, my mom told me that if I could play the piano, I would be the life of the party.

I never got good enough at the piano to live that out, but I'm working on the harmonica side of things.

I don't think the instrument matters, or even that there's an instrument involved. What matters is the illumination of the possibility—that in some way, I had the potential to be the life of the party, whatever form that party took.

In high school, I knew that party wouldn't look like a rave, maybe not even a typical high school party. Rich white kids in a Boston suburb didn't throw parties I wanted to breathe life into.

During my freshman year at the University of Maine, the life of the party looked like drunken dorm pregames before walking over to the hockey stadium. Videos of dick-shaped popsicles, mercifully timed before the advent of Instagram stories and TikTok.

I'm still trying to figure out what kind of party happened at the academy. Looking back, I always felt like a distant cousin at the wedding—welcome, but not part of the main event. Hard to be the life of the party there. Maybe it was the post-apocalyptic stumble onto the sands of Virginia Beach on a gray morning after a bender with kids a class up from me. Maybe it was sucking three Juuls at once on a late November night, trying to break the nicotine addiction. Maybe it was falling asleep wedged into the corner of an Airbnb balcony after another unrecallable, likely regrettable night. Not much of a party either way.

Maybe it was the game nights at the University of Florida, the brewery crawls, or the dance nights at the drag show. Warmer, but still not quite there yet.

In Colorado Springs, the Wednesday ride was the first time I felt like the life of the party. I'd spent half a decade trying and failing to find my own group, so I finally said "screw it" and made my own. At that point, life was moving so fast that I got speed wobbles and fell off the ride. I've written plenty about those months and won't bore you with the lore here. Anyway—in my absence, the Wednesday ride was quickly repackaged into a different form with a different face and lives on as a different kind of party.

Over the past year, I think I've found my groove. I followed the same playbook I used when I created the Wednesday ride. Loosely, it follows the logic of "build it and they will come." This time, I incorporated elements of evolved arachnid social interactions described by Adrian Tchaikovsky in *Children of Time*. Namely, creating social "webs." The web analogy is twofold: first, like the

Wednesday ride, the party relies on the use of a net, usually in the form of a standing event (exhibit A: the Espresso Express). Second, it requires frequent interconnection between members of the web. The social web is a formation of frequent interactions with other members of the group, just like the character Portia in *Children of Time*. I am the spider that is spinning the web. Fortunately, I don't have venom and won't liquefy the insides of people who join the party. In fact, I try to give a little more life to everyone who finds themselves in the web. I'm still trying to feel out whether that giving is a zero-sum game or not.

Either way, these are parties I'm happy to be the life of.

94

ACROSTIC 2

I want to tell you a short fable. Have a minute? Everything in it is made up. Someone else told it first. Could be someone you know. Want to hear?

But first, I want to draw your attention to the air around you. Feel it? No breeze, no movement. Sense the stillness. Of course, if you're outside, you might feel a breeze. Belonging to the space you're in is a beautiful feeling. Or simply being present without judgment.

Direction, it seems, finds us, rather than the other way around.

In a sense, we are all very much the same as the air we breathe. My fingers, my hands, my hair, my brain, all made up of the carbon I inhale. Life begets life. And we return the favor. I feel part of the world around me. Am I?

Near the finish line, but not quite there yet. My lungs burn, my legs churn. Breaking into new frontiers each day. Point me into the wind and let me go.

It seems like I forgot to get around to the fable. Now that I look at it, the first word in each sentence may offer a similar, but very different story.

95

HOW TO JUMP-START A SOUL

I poke a foot out and the cool air of the bedroom coats it in a reminder that the world still exists. I hit snooze and allow the covers to ensnare me again in a fragile cocoon.

The reluctance to face the world outweighs the logic of getting up with enough time to make myself a solid breakfast. I rush around the kitchen trying to cram two microwaved eggs in my mouth and lunch in my bag, and the whole time, I am standing in the doorway watching myself, still and unmoving. Observing my human body bustle around, all frustrated and unidirectional. Bored, I turn to the window and wait till it's time to go.

I arrive at work and go through the morning ritual. At some point in the autopilot of the day, I start to feel like myself again. Maybe it's the sunlight. Or the people. Perhaps it's the mechanical certainty of screws and threads and petroleum derivatives.

The end of the day brings a slam dunk of exhaustion as I

close the car door and sit for a moment. I have a splitting headache. There is sticky residue in my elbow creases, the kind that comes after nine hours in a metal box outside in the summer. A palpable heartache. Dehydration that I can feel in my gums. The spike of hunger, because the lunch I packed myself was simply insufficient.

The dishes wait for me in the sink, crusted with egg and yogurt and a piece of black plum skin. I make myself some rice in the instant pot and put the laundry in the dryer.

I pick up the guitar and record some music. It sounds like shit when I listen to it. Maybe I'll get an electric guitar.

96

SHINLEAF SYMPHONY

Gotta get it down fast
Four acts then I'm out. I haven't slept more than a few winks since Monday night..

act i: swim

> The hammock was strung up,
> the bike was locked up,
> the campsite was safe.
>
> I wandered down a ways
> and leveled my gaze
> out across the river.
>
> I hopped on in
> and started to swim
> and stopped when I'd crossed it.

I sat for a while,
watched the planes on final,
and the weight began to lift.

I swam back across,
stumbled up on some rocks,
and kept walking down the trail.

act ii: swing

I sat on the isthmus
and thought how much I'd missed this
since the last time I was here.

The sun and the sand
on that threadbare strand,
my eyes on the austral sky.

The wind whipped toward me,
the boats ignored me,
the clouds billowed and darkened.

I sat just the same
as the curtain of rain
marched across the water.

The droplets pelted,
my skin nearly welted,
I took cover in the trees.

act iii: nature

The storm was severe,
not a soul was near,
so I stripped down and walked naked.

The path lay before
and led to the shore,
so I followed it into the cove.

I swam out into the squall
and exhaled the fall
down into those cold green depths.

I sat on the sediment,
and high above, the storm went
on and on its madman ways.

I resurfaced and watched it pass
while the rain spun orbs of glass
on the ripples in the restless water.

act iv: night

The sunset burned sienna,
and with my harp, I tried to send a
tune across the river.

With my campfire desiccated
and my dinner preparated,
it came time for me to go to bed.

The hammock had dried,
and I found myself inside,
making it wet again—with my sweat glands.

A few minutes past midnight,
the whole forest turned light,
and a moment later, a deafening boom.

This storm was not typical,
it was frightening, it was biblical.
Freshly soaked, I tucked in for a long night.

97

HAIKU 42

Making a mistake
Just means you're doing something.
Keep doing something.

98

DEAR FRIEND

Dear friend,

I am finally getting around to this letter. I have thought about it a little since last weekend. I can't say I have come to any sort of earth-shattering revelation, but after mulling it all over in my noggin, I do feel like I have something to say.

I say it to you (or rather, write it to you) from a strange place. Not literally—I am on my living room floor, typing this on the Thursday typewriter (what a gem)—but rather, from a strange relational place.

Usually, I write letters to those closest to me—my family, my wife, and a small handful of friends, whom I've nurtured relationships with for years. However, you and I are not very close friends. You are close to and important to some of my closest friends, though, and I care about you.

You and I have not had a chance to grow our roots deeply. I think that's natural for two people on opposite corners of the foursquare, so to speak.

We have, however, been deeply hurt by those who are in our "in" groups. In your case, your family. In my case, the branch of the military I was briefly in.

Although I wasn't as committed to the Navy as one might be to their biological family, I was wholly part of the institution socially, emotionally, intellectually, morally, and my entire future was mapped out with the Navy at the center of it all.

Then, as those roots had grown just deep enough to commit me and the next five years of my life after graduation to naval service, I was ripped away from what I had grown into. I had commanders, captains, and a vice admiral come as close to literally spitting in my face as they could legally have come. Really—they probably could have. Their lawyers were in the room. Mine wasn't. Most of the others in the room, spectating the complete and utter demolition of my character, reputation, and self-worth, in that cruelly public forum, looked on in contempt and without mercy.

I left the Naval Academy with $138,000 of debt to the United States government and a black blemish on my professional record that even today I struggle to overcome. Moreso, I had a completely ruined vision of myself—who I was, am, and what I can offer the world. I was destroyed.

Most damaging, I hated the people who did it to me. I hated the words they wrote and said about me. "MIDN Zamot has no character." "MIDN Zamot has no integrity." "I fully recommend the separation of MIDN Zamot." "You are a predator."

Why am I saying all of this? What does this have to do with you?

In time, I forgave everyone who ever did wrong to me. It freed me up to so much light, happiness, and joy. It removed a weight from my soul that I harbored for years. I suffered, and I still do. But without holding that resentment in my heart, I have freed up space for a lot more joy.

I know you've been hurt. I can't imagine how awful it was or how much it still hurts you. But I think forgiveness holds a power that not much else does. A power to bring light into the dark corners of your soul. I hope that one day, you might find yourself in a position to forgive those who have hurt you.

Your friend,
Cameron

99

SO, WHAT DID YOU LEARN?

Last night at Electric Moon, Anastasia asked me, "What is the biggest thing you learned from the Naval Academy?"

I stared at her for a few seconds and realized that no one —absolutely no one—had ever asked me that in the past five years. Despite all the things I've written and said about my time there and its aftermath, no one had ever posed that question.

After she asked, I paused to think before giving her an answer. I'll start with that one here, then delve into a secondary lesson, and maybe even a third if I feel like it.

The primary lesson I learned is that, in civil societies, most people are allies. Those who don't end up being allies will probably become irrelevant because no one really has the authority to screw up your life. The basic takeaway is this: people are allies until proven otherwise, and if they aren't, they simply become irrelevant. At the academy, there were people I feared—people who could use their authority to inflict some kind of harm on me. They could control me on a deeper level than, say, an employer or a professor at a civilian university. I feared them because the institution, or "the system," gave them that power. But in the civilian world, those kinds of relationships don't exist. No other average human has the authority to instill that kind of fear in a civil setting because our civil institutions don't allow it.

Of course, if we cross into the realm of criminal acts, fear exists. Women, people of color, and other groups experience fear of rape or police brutality, for instance. But this is outside the scope of my argument, as those are crimes.

This philosophy of "allies until proven irrelevant" has a few advantages. For one, it reduces the anxiety I feel when talking to people I admire or those in positions of authority —whether that's a local power broker, a lawyer, a city council member, or a former county commissioner. Even if the conversation revolves around me and my seemingly wild idea that I need their help with, it doesn't faze me. Because ultimately, it's not about me; it's about them. But that's a topic for another blog.

Second, this philosophy aligns with a related idea: that the world can hurt us more than any individual person can. The trap of our modern globalist and capitalist society ensnares all of us. Though we've seen a decrease in criminal violence since the 1980s, this world still functions like a very comfortable prison. The systems we live in can inflict far more harm than any single person could.

The worst scenario I can imagine is being a homeless drug addict in a city. No one individual can do that to another person; it takes an entire system of failures to create even one homeless individual. Today, we see homelessness in droves throughout the country. The system has clearly failed.

Our only real lifelines are the connections we make with others. Salaries are not certain, nor are they lifelines; they come and go. If an entire bank, an entire state, or even a corporation can disappear, so too can a salary.

The only true lifeline in this broken world is a simple relationship with another person, multiplied many times over and spread across different geographic locations. This forms the net that keeps us protected from the world because the systems we live in can hurt us far more than any one person ever could.

100

35 ITEMS

I haven't been employed since November 14th, so I haven't really had the money to go anywhere or do much fun stuff besides the basics.

Since May, I've worked on weekends, and Lauren, with her day job, works during the week. So we are kind of in Raleigh the whole time. All the time, actually. All the fucking time.

And so, here are some of the boring things I've done in this boring little city since I haven't really left in November of last year:

- Started a business
- Learned how to play the harmonica (well-ish)
- Learned how to record music
- Learned how to play the guitar
- Learned how to play the keyboard

- Learned how to program an Arduino using ChatGPT
- Learned how to create a small robot controlled by an Arduino using ChatGPT
- Applied to 190 jobs
- Watched a movie about typewriters
- Bought two typewriters
- Wrote poetry
- Wrote grant proposals
- Met with city council members
- Spoke at a city council public comment session
- Helped revive a ride called Critical Mass
- Wrote letters
- Enjoyed a Friday morning coffee ride with my friends every Friday
- Cultivated a weekly Tuesday group ride—last week we had 29 members, up from 4 less than a year ago!
- Played harmonica in a live jam session
- Got married
- Graduated from my MBA program
- Had long walks and deep talks with my parents
- Rode my bike in the rain
- Attended the Raleigh Planning Academy
- Bought a kei van
- Wore a suit while driving that kei van to an interview with the Raleigh Police Department
- Didn't get the job
- Worked long, hot hours at the container on quiet, oppressive summer days

- Fixed bikes
- Listened to stories
- Rented bikes
- Made videos
- Drove my brother and sister-in-law to the airport as they headed overseas
- Hired an employee

I am not sure I'll get this job. But I probably won't stop doing stuff.

EDITOR'S NOTE

Somewhere after the last chapter, a colleague who knew Cameron well, who knew his passion and desire and determination and education, asked him to join the team, and make the City of Raleigh better for all.

Which means that he did, in fact, get the job.

ABOUT THE AUTHOR

Cameron Zamot's career path has been anything but ordinary. After earning his degree in Mechanical Engineering from the University of Florida in 2021, he started out knocking on doors selling solar panels, then transitioned to designing structural reinforcements for solar installations, and eventually found himself building e-learning courses on how to install them.

When tech industry layoffs brought an unexpected pause, Cameron seized the moment to start **The Bike Library** (www.thebikelibrary.com), a community hub promoting human-powered transportation. Operating weekends at NC State University's Centennial Campus, TBL has become a gathering place for cyclists and advocates alike.

Today, Cameron serves as the Executive Director of **Greenway Gear Collective** (www.greenwaygearcollective.org), a nonprofit focused on bike education and advocacy. When he's not riding bikes or championing cycling initiatives, you'll find him writing, playing the harmonica, or savoring a *cortado*.

Cameron also holds an MBA from the University of

Arizona and is a proud member of the American Planning Association (APA). He lives in Raleigh, NC, with his wife Lauren—a fellow Gator, MBA, bike enthusiast, and talented painter.

This is his first book.

The Bike Library

Greenway Gear Collective

🅞 instagram.com/the.bike.library

www.ingramcontent.com/pod-product-compliance
Lightning Source LLC
Chambersburg PA
CBHW030448100526
44580CB00002B/27